Better Homes and Gardens®

Our seal assures you that every recipe in *Eat and Stay Slim*
has been tested in the Better Homes and Gardens® Test Kitchen.
This means that each recipe is practical and reliable,
and meets our high standards of taste appeal.

BETTER HOMES AND GARDENS. BOOKS

Editor: Gerald M. Knox
Art Director: Ernest Shelton
Managing Editor: David A. Kirchner
Project Editors: James D. Blume, Marsha Jahns
Project Managers: Liz Anderson, Jennifer Speer Ramundt,
    Angela K. Renkoski

Food and Family Life Editor: Sharyl Heiken
Associate Department Editors: Sandra Granseth,
    Rosemary C. Hutchinson, Elizabeth Woolever
Senior Food Editors: Linda Henry, Mary Jo Plutt, Joyce Trollope
Associate Food Editors: Jennifer Darling, Debra-Ann Duggan,
    Heather M. Hephner, Mary Major, Shelli McConnell
Test Kitchen: Director, Sharon Stilwell; Photo Studio Director,
    Janet Herwig; Home Economists: Lynn Blanchard, Kay Cargill,
    Marilyn Cornelius, Maryellyn Krantz, Jennifer Nuese,
    Marge Steenson, Colleen Weeden

Associate Art Directors: Neoma Thomas, Linda Ford Vermie,
    Randall Yontz
Assistant Art Directors: Lynda Haupert, Harijs Priekulis,
    Tom Wegner
Graphic Designers: Mary Schlueter Bendgen, Michael Burns,
    Mick Schnepf
Art Production: Director, John Berg; Associate, Joe Heuer;
    Office Manager, Michaela Lester

President, Book Group: Jeramy Lanigan
Vice President, Retail Marketing: Jamie Martin
Vice President, Administrative Services: Rick Rundall

BETTER HOMES AND GARDENS. MAGAZINE
President, Magazine Group: James A. Autry
Editorial Director: Doris Eby
Food and Nutrition Editor: Nancy Byal

MEREDITH CORPORATION OFFICERS
Chairman of the Executive Committee: E. T. Meredith III
Chairman of the Board: Robert A. Burnett
President and Chief Executive Officer: Jack D. Rehm

EAT AND STAY SLIM

Editor: Mary Major
Editorial Project Manager: Liz Anderson
Graphic Designer: Lynda Haupert
Electronic Text Processors: Paula Forest, Mary Mathews
Contributing Food Stylists: Suzanne Finley, Carol Grones
Contributing Photographers: Sean Fitzgerald, Michael Jensen
Contributing Nutrition Consultant: Roberta L. Duyff, M.S., R.D.

On the cover: *Sweet Pepper and Turkey Rolls* (see recipe,
    page 30) and *Wild Rice and Mushrooms* (see recipe, page 90).

Contents

4   Introduction

5   Designing Your Weight-Loss Plan

8   Food Exchange Groups

12   Using the Daily Menu Plans

19   Main Dishes

71   Side Dishes

93   Desserts

103   Snacks

111   Nutrition and Weight Loss

113   Exercise

114   How to Stay Slim

115   Food Exchange Lists

121   Exchanges for Packaged Foods

127   Index

$\mathcal{S}$hed pounds while enjoying a variety of foods and without counting a single calorie. Sound too good to be true? It's not. With *Eat & Stay Slim,* you lose weight by keeping track of Food Exchanges, instead of counting calorie after calorie.

Here's how it works. To begin, choose one of our Daily Menu Plans that meets your weight-loss needs. Your plan lists the number of Food Exchanges you can enjoy at each meal. Then, fit recipes from this book and other foods you like into your plan.

From the following 140 delicious recipes, choose taste-tempting entrées, such as *Steak with Marsala Sauce* or *Garlic-Marinated Swordfish Steaks.* For dessert, bite into luscious but low-calorie *Mint-Chocolate Cream Puffs.* You also will find a wide variety of side-dish and snack recipes.

The best time to start your weight-loss diet is now. So, read on to learn more about this sensible approach to successful reducing.

Designing Your Weight-Loss Plan

You want to lose weight. But where do you start? First, set smart, realistic goals. Next, determine your daily caloric needs and choose a Daily Menu Plan that's right for you. Then, select recipes from this book, along with other foods, that fit into your Daily Menu Plan. Read on to discover how to handle each step.

Setting Your Goals

How much should you weigh? That depends on your age, height, body type, and sex. There's no absolute answer, but the Height/Weight Chart on page 7 offers some guidelines. Generally speaking, your weight as an older adult should be about the same as when you were 25 years old. If you were overweight as a young adult, your weight should probably be less.

Sensible goal setting is "health wise" and likely to result in permanent weight loss. Refer to these points when setting your goals:

■ Set realistic, achievable goals. Make your weight goal healthful, not unreasonably slim. If you need help, ask a registered dietitian or other health expert for assistance or advice.
■ Allow for gradual weight change. Plan to lose one to two pounds per week—the maximum rate that most doctors think is desirable and healthful without close medical supervision.
■ Establish short-term goals, as well as a target goal. You will feel good tracking your progress and reaching one weight-loss goal after another. Carefully set, short-term goals can lead to long-term success.
■ Reward your successes, both big and small, but never reward yourself with food. Instead, buy yourself a bouquet of flowers, choose a new

perfume or after-shave, or go to a movie when you reach a short-term goal. Treat yourself to a new outfit or a complete make-over when you reach your target goal.

Figuring Your Daily Caloric Needs

How many calories do you need each day to reach your weight goal? Losing, gaining, or maintaining weight is a matter of caloric arithmetic. When you consume more calories than your body burns, you gain weight. When you consume fewer, you lose weight. And when your caloric intake equals your caloric expenditure, your weight remains the same.

A pound of body fat contains about 3,500 calories, about the same number as in a pound of butter or margarine. So figure the arithmetic of reducing this way: Eat 3,500 fewer calories than your body uses, and shed 1 pound of body fat. Take in 7,000 fewer calories and lose 2 pounds!

How does that translate into everyday living? By consuming 1,000 fewer calories per day than you burn up, you should lose about 2 pounds in a week. Or, cut out only 500 calories per day and lose 1 pound per week. You can do that by consuming fewer calories, burning more calories or, better yet, doing both.

Most moderately active people need to consume about 15 calories per pound to maintain weight. For example, to keep from gaining or losing, a 133-pound woman needs 15 calories times 133, or 1,995 calories per day. To lose five pounds in five weeks, she should trim 500 calories from her diet each day:

1,995 maintenance calories per day
minus
500 calories per day
equals
1,495 calories per day in a reducing diet

(use 1,500-calorie Daily Menu Plan)

Remember, you can burn additional calories by increasing the amount of exercise you do each day. A moderate 30-minute walk burns about 100 calories. Keep it up every day for five weeks, and subtract 3,500 calories—the equivalent of one pound of body fat.

Your Daily Menu Plan

A diet is easy, flexible, and healthful when you use Food Exchanges and one of the Daily Menu Plans to guide you.

Health experts recommend a diet for adults that provides about 55 percent of total daily calories from carbohydrates, about 15 percent calories from protein, and about 30 percent calories from fat. The Daily Menu Plans in this book meet these guidelines and provide a variety of foods.

Choose the Daily Menu Plan that's right for you—one that lets you lose, then maintain weight. Here's how:

Calculate the daily caloric budget—1,000, 1,200, 1,500, 1,800 calories—that will help you lose no more than 2 pounds per week. A diet should never go below 800 calories per day without medical supervision.
Then, following the Daily Menu Plan that meets your caloric budget, choose from the recipes in this book and the foods from each of the Food Exchange groups.
Include exercise in your weight-loss plan. Successful, long-term weight control includes eating less and exercising more. Moreover, exercise leads to overall better health.
Ask a registered dietitian or other health professional if you have questions about your Daily Menu Plan, caloric needs, weight-loss goals, or exercise program.

What Is a Food Exchange?

Simply put, a Food Exchange is a measure of caloric and nutrient values. Foods are divided (according to their carbohydrate, protein, fat, and caloric content) into six Exchange Groups and a seventh group of Free Foods.

The term "exchange" means just that. Within each Food Exchange Group you can pick and choose among a wide variety of "equal" foods and beverages. ("Equal" means that the calories and nutrient values are similar, but not exactly the same.) If you meet your Food Exchange "budget," without going over, you're assured of a well-balanced diet within caloric limits.

To make meal planning easy, each Food Exchange Group is color coded for easy recognition. Eaten in adequate but moderate amounts, these foods form the framework of a healthful, appealing diet. The Exchange Groups and their colors are:

- ■ Starch/Bread Exchange
- ■ Meat Exchange
- ■ Vegetable Exchange
- ■ Fruit Exchange
- ■ Milk Exchange
- ■ Fat Exchange

Using Recipes and Food Exchanges in Daily Menu Plans

Your Daily Menu Plan states the number of exchanges from each group you may consume. Eating the right amount of food is essential. For this reason, the recipes give a specific number of servings, and the Food Exchange Charts on pages 115 to 120 define a specific amount of each food per exchange. Serving sizes will differ.

Most recipes in this book include exchanges from two or more groups. For example, Quick Chicken Cacciatore (see recipe, page 24) includes 3 Lean Meat Exchanges and 1 Vegetable Exchange. To make planning meals easier, a list of exchanges appears with each recipe. Subtract the exchanges for the recipe you choose from the total listed for the meal in your Daily Menu Plan. Then, select items from the Food Exchange Charts (see pages 115–120) for the remaining exchanges.

IDEAL HEIGHT AND WEIGHT

HEIGHT	SMALL FRAME	MEDIUM FRAME	LARGE FRAME
women			
4'10"	102–111	109–121	118–131
4'11"	103–113	111–123	120–134
5'0"	104–115	113–126	122–137
5'1"	106–118	115–129	125–140
5'2"	108–121	118–132	128–143
5'3"	111–124	121–135	131–147
5'4"	114–127	124–138	134–151
5'5"	117–130	127–141	137–155
5'6"	120–133	130–144	140–159
5'7"	123–136	133–147	143–163
5'8"	126–139	136–150	146–167
5'9"	129–142	139–153	149–170
5'10"	132–145	142–156	152–173
5'11"	135–148	145–159	155–176
6'0"	138–151	148–162	158–179
men			
5'2"	128–134	131–141	138–150
5'3"	130–136	133–143	140–153
5'4"	132–138	135–145	142–156
5'5"	134–140	137–148	144–160
5'6"	136–142	139–151	146–164
5'7"	138–145	142–154	149–168
5'8"	140–148	145–157	152–172
5'9"	142–151	148–160	155–176
5'10"	144–154	151–163	158–180
5'11"	146–157	154–166	161–184
6'0"	149–160	157–170	164–188
6'1"	152–164	160–174	168–192
6'2"	155–168	164–178	172–197
6'3"	158–172	167–182	176–202
6'4"	162–176	171–187	181–207

This table was issued in 1983 by the Metropolitan Life Insurance Company and is based on the weights of policyholders with the fewest illnesses and longest lives. Heights were measured in shoes with 1-inch heels, and weights with five pounds of indoor clothing (for men) and 3 pounds of indoor clothing (for women). These figures represent population averages; your ideal weight may differ.

Here's an overview of the six Food Exchange Groups. For a complete list of foods in each group and a list of Free Foods, see pages 115 to 120.

Meat Exchange

Meat, poultry, fish, eggs, cheese, peanut butter, and tofu belong on the Meat Exchange list because they are excellent protein sources. One exchange provides about 7 grams of protein. However, meats and meat alternates vary in the amount of fat and calories they contain. For this reason Meat Exchanges are divided into three categories—Lean, Medium-Fat, and High-Fat. See page 115 for an explanation on figuring the different Meat Exchanges into your diet. Most Meat Exchanges are based on 1 ounce of cooked meat. As a rule of thumb, 4 ounces of raw meat equals about 3 ounces of cooked meat.

Starch/Bread Exchange

A Starch/Bread Exchange can range from a baked potato to a tortilla. One serving of foods on this list (cereals, grains, pastas, dried beans, starchy vegetables, and breads) has about 15 grams of carbohydrate, 3 grams of protein, a small amount of fat, and 80 calories. Many Starch/Bread Exchanges, particularly dried beans and whole-grain and bran products, are good fiber sources. Many are also good sources of B vitamins and iron. Although serving sizes vary, use this guideline for unlisted foods: One exchange equals 1 ounce of bread or ½ cup of cereal or cooked pasta.

Fruit Exchange

Sweetened by nature, fruit is a perfect snack or menu item for weight-conscious individuals who desire something sweet. Fruits are a good source of vitamins A and C and potassium, yet contain no fat or protein. One Fruit Exchange supplies about 60 calories and 15 grams of carbohydrate. When using canned or frozen fruit, choose unsweetened varieties. Otherwise, you'll add unwanted calories. Fresh, dried, and frozen fruit are good fiber sources. Most Fruit Exchanges equal ½ cup of fresh or canned fruit or fruit juice, or ¼ cup of dried fruit.

Vegetable Exchange

Enjoy vegetables often because they're low-calorie, no-fat sources of vitamins, minerals, and fiber. One Vegetable Exchange contains about 5 grams of carbohydrate, 2 grams of protein, 25 calories, and 2 to 3 grams of fiber. One Vegetable Exchange is provided by ½ cup of cooked vegetables or vegetable juice, or 1 cup of raw vegetables. Some vegetables, such as lettuce, cucumbers, and mushrooms, are so low in calories that they are Free Foods. Because others are high in starch (dried beans, corn, peas, and potatoes) they're on the Starch/Bread Exchange list.

Milk Exchange

Milk and milk products are excellent sources of calcium, the nutrient needed for strong, healthy bones. One Milk Exchange contains about 12 grams of carbohydrate and 8 grams of protein. However, the amounts of milk fat and calories differ per exchange. Skim milk products are lowest in calories. They are almost fat free or contain less than ½ percent milk fat. Low-fat milk products have slightly more fat and calories. When buying milk products, check labels to determine the fat and calorie content.

Fat Exchange

Fats can be a deceptive group of foods. They pack plenty of calories into beguiling, small parcels. Often hidden in foods, calorie-dense fats can add extra pounds quickly if you aren't watchful. So measure them carefully. Each Fat Exchange provides about 5 grams of fat, 45 calories, and, for some items, a small amount of protein. Check package labels to identify products that contain higher levels of sodium. Unsaturated and saturated fats are listed separately. Limit saturated fat, which tends to raise blood cholesterol in some people.

Using the Daily Menu Plans

Now that you know your calorie budget and have become familiar with Food Exchanges, you are ready to start planning your meals using your Daily Menu Plan.

Forget counting calories. Instead of counting calories, keep track of Food Exchanges and the calories will take care of themselves. Following your Daily Menu Plan, just eat the right number of servings from each Food Exchange (without nibbling on extras). Your calorie intake will be right on target.

Four Daily Menu Plans appear on pages 15–18. Take a look at the plan that provides the number of calories—1,000, 1,200, 1,500, or 1,800 calories—for your rate of weight loss. (The number of calories you need is based on your calculations from page 5.) Examining your Daily Menu Plan, see how many exchanges from each group you can enjoy at each meal.

Planning Meals

Plan all your meals for an entire day at one time to keep your exchanges balanced throughout the day. You may find it pays to plan meals for several days at once, since you will simplify counting exchanges, grocery shopping, and cooking. Remember the menus that you like or that work well in your time schedule and use them again. Meal planning will become easier once you have some tried-and-true menus.

Each Daily Menu Plan provides for three meals a day. If you want to plan for a snack, borrow some Food Exchanges from one of the meals, or fill up on Free Foods. Or, you may want to divide your Food Exchanges into several mini-meals.

Choose the foods you like from the recipes in this book and the color-coded Food Exchange Lists (see pages 115–120), using your exchange budget. Remember, you can substitute one food for another in the same Food Exchange List, but you can't swap from one list to another.

Balancing Your Meals

At any meal, you may skip an exchange or two. Be sure to make up for it at another meal or enjoy it as a snack later in the day. This assures that you are receiving all the nutrients you need to maintain your health while you lose weight.

At other times, you may want to add an extra exchange to a meal. Subtract this exchange from one of your other meals that day so you don't consume too many calories, which will slow your weight loss.

Figuring Meat and Milk Exchanges

Foods on the Meat and Milk Exchange Lists vary significantly in the amount of fat they contain. For this reason, both of these groups are divided into subcategories. Here's how each group works in your Daily Menu Plan.

Meats and their alternates are divided into Lean, Medium-Fat, and High-Fat subcategories. But, the Daily Menu Plans are written for Lean Meat Exchanges. When you eat a Medium-Fat Meat Exchange, charge yourself one Lean Meat Exchange and one-half Fat Exchange. Each High-Fat Meat Exchange costs one Lean Meat Exchange and an additional Fat Exchange. For the recipes in this book, the Medium-Fat and High-Fat Meat Exchanges have been converted to Lean Meat and Fat Exchanges.

Although the Milk Exchange list is divided into skim, low-fat, and whole subcategories, the Daily Menu Plans are written for skim milk products. For low-fat products, charge yourself one Milk Exchange plus one-half Fat Exchange. For whole milk products, count one Milk Exchange plus one Fat Exchange.

Mixed Exchanges

"Mixed" foods, such as stews, casseroles, and many of the recipes in this book, combine foods from two or more of the Exchange Lists. For recipes in this book, Food Exchanges have been calculated and appear after each recipe.

You will find many prepared and convenience foods listed on the chart titled "Exchanges for Packaged Foods" on page 121.

For unlisted foods or your own recipes, estimate exchanges by determining what portion of an exchange each ingredient represents. For example, a serving of stew may contain 2 ounces of cooked lean beef (2 Lean Meat Exchanges), ½ cup of potato (1 Starch/Bread Exchange), and ½ cup carrots (1 Vegetable Exchange).

Alcohol Calories Do Count

It's OK to enjoy an alcoholic drink now and then even though it doesn't belong in a Food Exchange Group. If you consume alcoholic beverages, drink in moderation. And, be aware of the calorie consequences. Because even one drink adds unwanted calories and no nutrients, it will take you over your calorie budget. For example, while providing no nutritional value, 8 ounces of beer provide 114 calories; light beer has slightly less. One jigger (1½ ounces) of 90-proof liquor supplies about 110 calories. And, table wine has about 87 calories per 3½ ounces. Dry wines have fewer calories than sweet wines.

MEAL PLANNING STEP-BY-STEP

Take meal planning one step at a time and see how simple it is. Here are seven easy steps:

- For each meal, start with a main dish that is within your exchange guidelines for the meal. It might be just meat, poultry, or fish, or it might be a recipe from this book. If you choose three ounces of broiled fish, mark off three Lean Meat Exchanges. If you choose a recipe, you may have used three Lean Meat Exchanges plus one Vegetable Exchange.
- Select a Starch/Bread Exchange. If you choose rice, for example, allow yourself ⅓ cup of cooked rice and check off one exchange.
- Choose a Fruit Exchange as a side dish or dessert and mark it off.
- How many Vegetable Exchanges can you allow yourself? If you have two exchanges, you may choose ½ cup green beans and one large broiled tomato.
- Add a Milk Exchange, unless you have used it in cooking.
- Decide on any Fat Exchanges not used in cooking. One teaspoon margarine on the rice equals one Fat Exchange. Six dry-roasted almonds tossed on the green beans add one more Fat Exchange.
- Add Free Foods as desired. Coffee or tea might accompany the dessert.

	S	M	T	W	T	F	S	S	M	T	W	T	F	S

BREAKFAST

LUNCH

DINNER

■ **MEAT** ■ **STARCH/BREAD** ■ **FRUIT**
■ **VEGETABLES** ■ **MILK** ■ **FAT**

Keeping Tabs On Yourself

Draw up a work sheet (like the one shown at *left*) to help you keep track of the foods you eat. Tuck it into your purse or wallet and you'll know exactly how many exchanges you've used for the day.

Select a way to represent each Exchange Group. In our sample chart (*below*), we colored in the squares to correspond to the colors that represent the Exchange Groups in this book. Use colored pencils or felt-tipped pens to fill in your squares.

Check off the exchanges you consume as you eat each meal or snack. At any one meal, you may eat a few extra exchanges or you may not eat all the exchanges you are allowed. But, by the end of the day, your total exchange consumption should equal your total exchange allowance. Review the sample menus on pages 15–18 to see how this works.

Color the exchanges allowed for each meal →

Check off the exchanges as you → use them

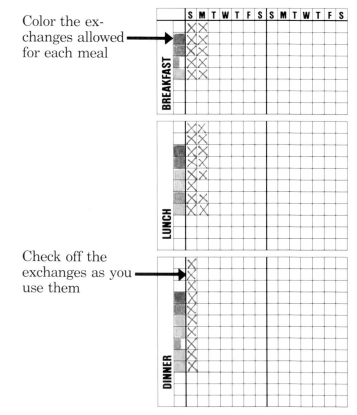

1,000 Calorie Daily Menu Plan

The exchange allotments for each meal appear in the top row of the chart. Count the squares of each color to determine the number from each Exchange Group allowed for each meal.

■ MEAT ■ STARCH/BREAD ■ FRUIT
■ VEGETABLES ■ MILK ■ FAT

	BREAKFAST EXCHANGES ■ ■ ■ ■ ■	LUNCH EXCHANGES ■ ■ ■ ■ ■	DINNER EXCHANGES ■ ■ ■ ■ ■ ■
SAMPLE MENU A	■ ■ 1 ounce cheddar cheese on ½ toasted bagel ■ 1 sliced kiwi fruit ■ ½ cup skim milk	■ ■ 2 ounces sliced lean roast beef on 2 very thin slices bread with 1 tablespoon reduced-calorie mayonnaise ■ ■ Creamy Asparagus Soup* Sugar-free soft drink	■ ■ ■ Hot Chicken Salad* ■ 1 small roll with 1 teaspoon margarine ■ 1¼ cups strawberries ■ 1 cup skim milk
SAMPLE MENU B	■ 1 poached egg ■ ½ toasted English muffin with 1 teaspoon margarine ■ 1 cup raspberries ■ ½ cup skim milk	■ ■ Ham Burritos* ■ Carrot sticks cut from 1 medium carrot ■ 1 cup skim milk	■ Poached Fish with Lime Sauce* ■ Pepper-Rice Timbales* ■ ½ cup cooked broccoli ■ 1 cup salad greens tossed with 2 tablespoons reduced-calorie salad dressing ■ 1 peach ■ ½ cup skim milk

*For recipe, see index.

1,200 Calorie Daily Menu Plan

The exchange allotments for each meal appear in the top row of the chart. Count the squares of each color to determine the number from each Exchange Group allowed for each meal.

■ MEAT ■ STARCH/BREAD ■ FRUIT
■ VEGETABLES ■ MILK ■ FAT

	BREAKFAST EXCHANGES ■ ■ ■ ■ ■	LUNCH EXCHANGES ■ ■ ■ ■ ■ ■ ■	DINNER EXCHANGES ■ ■ ■ ■ ■ ■ ■ ■
SAMPLE MENU A	■ ■ 1 egg fried in nonstick spray coating ■ 1 slice toast with 2 teaspoons sugar-free jelly ■ ¾ cup blueberries ■ ½ cup skim milk	■ ■ ■ Tuna Toss* ■ 1-ounce slice French bread with 1 teaspoon margarine ■ ½ cup cooked green beans sprinkled with 1 tablespoon Parmesan cheese ■ 1 apple ■ 1 cup skim milk	■ ■ ■ Tex-Mex Turkey Tenderloins* ■ ⅓ cup cooked rice with 1 teaspoon margarine ■ ■ ¾ cup cooked mixed cauliflower and broccoli ■ ⅛ avocado, sliced ■ 1 cup sliced papaya ■ ½ cup skim milk
SAMPLE MENU B	■ ¼ cup low-fat cottage cheese ■ ■ Orange-Applesauce Muffin* ■ ⅓ cup canned pineapple cubes ■ ½ cup skim milk	■ ■ ■ Fruited Chicken Salad* ■ Herbed Tomato Juice* ■ ■ ¾ cup steamed pea pods ■ 1 small roll with 1 teaspoon margarine ■ 1 plum ■ 1 cup skim milk	■ ■ ■ Roast Beef with Mushroom Sauce* ■ ½ cup steamed asparagus ■ ½ cup cooked carrots ■ 1 cup salad greens tossed with 2 tablespoons reduced-calorie salad dressing ■ ½ cup mashed potatoes with 1 teaspoon margarine ■ Fresh Fruit Plate* ■ ½ cup skim milk

For recipe, see index.

1,500 Calorie Daily Menu Plan

The exchange allotments for each meal appear in the top row of the chart. Count the squares of each color to determine the number from each Exchange Group allowed for each meal.

■ MEAT ■ STARCH/BREAD ■ FRUIT
■ VEGETABLES ■ MILK ■ FAT

	BREAKFAST EXCHANGES	LUNCH EXCHANGES	DINNER EXCHANGES
SAMPLE MENU A	Eggs Florentine* ½ English muffin with 1 teaspoon margarine ½ grapefruit ½ cup skim milk	2½ ounces cooked turkey and 2 slices tomato and 1 tablespoon reduced-calorie mayonnaise on 2 slices rye bread Calorie-Counter's Coleslaw* 5 small olives ½ cup canned apricots 1 cup skim milk	Cajun Pork Pinwheels* 1 square cornbread with 1 teaspoon margarine ¾ cup steamed summer squash ½ cup unsweetened applesauce Pumpkin Chiffon Pudding* Carbonated water
SAMPLE MENU B	½ cup bran flakes with ½ cup skim milk 1 slice toast with 1 teaspoon margarine ½ cup apple juice	Taco Compuesto* Creamy Vegetable Toss* ⅛ honeydew melon 1 cup skim milk	Cheese-Stuffed Chicken Breasts* 1 small baked potato with 1½ teaspoons margarine 1 small roll with 1 teaspoon margarine ½ cup cooked broccoli Marinated Tomatoes and Cucumbers* Tropical Fruit Cup* ½ cup skim milk

*For recipe, see index.

1,800 Calorie Daily Menu Plan

The exchange allotments for each meal appear in the top row of the chart. Count the squares of each color to determine the number from each Exchange Group allowed for each meal.

■ MEAT ■ STARCH/BREAD ■ FRUIT
■ VEGETABLES ■ MILK ■ FAT

	BREAKFAST EXCHANGES	LUNCH EXCHANGES	DINNER EXCHANGES

SAMPLE MENU A

Breakfast
- Two 1-ounce slices Canadian bacon
- 2 waffles topped with 1 cup cut-up fresh fruit
- ½ cup skim milk

Lunch
- Taco Chicken Stew*
- 1 slice French bread with 1 teaspoon margarine
- 1 cup skim milk

Dinner
- Creamy Chive Dip*
- Veal Chops with Vegetables*
- 1 cup salad greens tossed with 2 tablespoons reduced-calorie salad dressing
- 1 small baked potato with 1½ teaspoons margarine
- 2 breadsticks
- ½ cup cooked brussels sprouts
- Pear-Date Crisp*
- 1 cup skim milk

SAMPLE MENU B

Breakfast
- Salsa Frittata*
- 2 slices toast with 2 teaspoons margarine
- 15 grapes
- ½ cup skim milk

Lunch
- 1½ ounces lean baked ham with 1 ounce Swiss cheese with 1 tablespoon reduced-calorie mayonnaise on 2 slices rye bread
- Herbed Tomato Soup*
- 6 saltine crackers
- 1 nectarine
- 1 cup skim milk

Dinner
- Lime Beef-and-Chicken Kabobs*
- ⅓ cup brown rice with 1 teaspoon margarine
- ½ cup cooked broccoli
- 1 small roll with 1 teaspoon margarine
- Melon Mousse*
- 1 cup skim milk

*For recipe, see index.

Main Dishes

Feature these savory stir-fries, steamy stews, refreshing salads, and flavorful kabobs in your weight-loss meals. Even nondieters will find them satisfying and delicious.

COUNTRY FRENCH CHICKEN

Pair this herbed chicken dish with boiled new potatoes. (Count the potatoes as Bread Exchanges.)

2 pounds meaty chicken pieces (breast halves, thighs, drumsticks)
  Nonstick spray coating
1 cup sliced fresh mushrooms
1 cup sliced celery
1 cup dry white wine
½ cup coarsely chopped carrot
1 medium onion, cut into small wedges
1 clove garlic, minced
1 bay leaf
2 tablespoons snipped parsley
¼ teaspoon dried thyme, crushed

Remove skin from chicken. Rinse chicken; pat dry. Spray a *cold* large skillet with nonstick coating. Preheat the skillet over medium heat. Brown chicken on all sides in hot skillet. Drain fat from skillet.

Season chicken lightly with salt and pepper. Add mushrooms, celery, white wine, carrot, onion, garlic, bay leaf, parsley, and thyme to the skillet. Bring to boiling; reduce heat. Cover and simmer for 35 to 40 minutes or till chicken is tender and no longer pink. Discard bay leaf. Transfer chicken and vegetables to a serving platter; keep warm.

For sauce, bring liquid in skillet to boiling. Cook about 3 minutes or till reduced to ½ cup. Pour sauce over chicken and vegetables. Makes 6 servings. One serving equals:

■ ■ ■ **Lean Meat Exchanges**
■ **Vegetable Exchange**

BAKED CAJUN CHICKEN

For honest-to-goodness Cajun flavor, use the larger amounts of the white, black, and red pepper.

1½ to 2 pounds meaty chicken pieces (breast halves, thighs, drumsticks)
  Nonstick spray coating
2 tablespoons skim milk
½ teaspoon onion powder
½ teaspoon dried thyme, crushed
¼ teaspoon garlic salt
⅛ to ¼ teaspoon ground white pepper
⅛ to ¼ teaspoon ground red pepper
⅛ to ¼ teaspoon ground black pepper

Remove skin from chicken. Rinse chicken; pat dry. Spray a 13x9x2-inch baking dish with nonstick coating. Arrange the chicken, meaty sides up, in dish. Brush with milk.

In a small bowl mix onion powder, thyme, garlic salt, white pepper, red pepper, and black pepper. Sprinkle over chicken.

Bake in a 375° oven for 45 to 55 minutes or till the chicken is tender and no longer pink. Makes 4 servings. One serving equals:

■ ■ ■ **Lean Meat Exchanges**

To skin drumsticks, cut a slit in the skin with a knife. Then, pull the skin away from the meat.

CHINESE-STYLE CHICKEN

The meaty chicken pieces simmer in a mixture of sherry and soy sauce.

1½ to 2 pounds meaty chicken pieces (breast halves, thighs, drumsticks)
   Nonstick spray coating
¾ cup water
2 tablespoons dry sherry
2 tablespoons reduced-sodium soy sauce
⅛ teaspoon garlic powder
2 tablespoons water
1 tablespoon cornstarch
1 cup bias-sliced celery (¼ inch thick)
4 green onions, cut into 1-inch pieces
1⅓ cups hot cooked rice

Remove skin from chicken. Rinse chicken; pat dry. Spray a *cold* large skillet with nonstick coating. Preheat the skillet over medium heat. Brown chicken pieces on all sides in hot skillet.

Add ¾ cup water, sherry, soy sauce, and garlic powder. Bring to boiling; reduce heat. Simmer, covered, for 35 to 40 minutes or till chicken is tender and no longer pink. Transfer chicken to a serving platter; keep warm.

For sauce, stir together the 2 tablespoons water and the cornstarch; set aside. Add celery and green onions to skillet. Cook and stir for 3 to 4 minutes or till celery is crisp-tender. Stir in cornstarch mixture. Cook and stir till thickened and bubbly. Cook and stir for 2 minutes more. Serve chicken and sauce with hot cooked rice. Makes 4 servings. One serving equals:

▪ ▪ ▪ **Lean Meat Exchanges**
▪ **Starch/Bread Exchange**

SPICY BAKED CHICKEN

Bake this slimming, oven-fried chicken till the herb-flavored coating is golden brown and crispy.

1½ to 2 pounds meaty chicken pieces (breast halves, thighs, drumsticks)
⅓ cup fine dry bread crumbs
2 tablespoons snipped parsley
¾ teaspoon dried Italian seasoning, crushed
½ teaspoon seasoned salt *or* salt
⅛ teaspoon ground red pepper
¼ cup all-purpose flour
3 tablespoons skim milk
   Nonstick spray coating

Remove skin from chicken. Rinse chicken; pat dry.

In a medium mixing bowl stir together bread crumbs, snipped parsley, Italian seasoning, seasoned salt or salt, and ground red pepper.

Place flour in a plastic bag. Place milk in a shallow bowl; set aside. Add chicken pieces, one at a time, to the bag; shake to coat. Dip in milk; then, dip in bread crumb mixture, pressing lightly to coat well.

Spray a 13x9x2-inch baking dish with nonstick coating. Arrange chicken pieces, meaty sides up, in the dish. Bake in a 375° oven for 45 to 55 minutes or till chicken is tender and no longer pink. Makes 4 servings. One serving equals:

▪ ▪ ▪ **Lean Meat Exchanges**
▪ **Starch/Bread Exchange**

Hot Chicken Salad

HOT CHICKEN SALAD

Apple juice is paired with vinegar to make a sweet-and-sour dressing for this wilted salad.

8 ounces cooked chicken *or* turkey
¼ cup apple juice
¼ cup vinegar
2 tablespoons sliced green onions
2 tablespoons water
1 teaspoon cornstarch
¼ teaspoon salt
¼ teaspoon dry mustard
¼ teaspoon celery seed
   Dash pepper
   Nonstick spray coating
4 cups torn fresh spinach
3 cups shredded cabbage
½ cup sliced radishes
2 whole radishes (optional)
   Celery leaves (optional)

Cut chicken or turkey into bite-size strips. For dressing, stir together apple juice, vinegar, green onions, water, cornstarch, salt, mustard, celery seed, and pepper; set aside.

Spray a *cold* 12-inch skillet with nonstick coating. Preheat the skillet over medium heat. Add chicken or turkey to skillet. Cook and stir for 1 to 2 minutes or till heated.

Add dressing to skillet. Cook and stir till thickened and bubbly. Cook and stir for 2 minutes more.

Toss together spinach and cabbage. Add to skillet. Cook and stir about 1 minute or till spinach starts to wilt. Add sliced radishes; toss to mix. Transfer to a salad bowl. If desired, garnish with whole radishes and celery leaves. Serve immediately. Makes 4 (2-cup) servings. One serving equals:

   Lean Meat Exchanges
   Vegetable Exchange

CHICKEN AND BROCCOLI SKILLET

These boneless chicken breasts are perfectly seasoned with garlic, lemon pepper, and thyme.

   Nonstick spray coating
2 cups broccoli cut into ¾-inch pieces
½ cup chopped onion
¼ teaspoon lemon pepper
¼ teaspoon dried thyme, crushed
2 teaspoons cooking oil
1 clove garlic, minced
4 boned skinless chicken breast halves
   (1 pound total)
1 cup halved cherry tomatoes

Spray a *cold* large skillet with nonstick coating. Preheat skillet over medium heat. Add broccoli, onion, lemon pepper, and thyme to skillet. Cook and stir for 3 to 4 minutes or till vegetables are crisp-tender. Remove vegetable mixture from the skillet; keep warm.

Add oil and garlic to hot skillet. Rinse chicken; pat dry. Add to skillet. Cook chicken over medium-high heat about 10 minutes or till chicken is tender and no longer pink, turning once. Return the vegetable mixture to skillet. Add cherry tomatoes. Cover and cook for 1 to 2 minutes or till heated through. Makes 4 servings. One serving equals:

   Lean Meat Exchanges
   Vegetable Exchange
   Fat Exchange

23

QUICK CHICKEN CACCIATORE

We borrowed traditional Italian flavors, but used boned chicken breast halves to hasten cooking.

4 **boned skinless chicken breast halves (1 pound total)**
1 **7½-ounce can tomatoes, cut up**
¾ **cup sliced fresh mushrooms**
¼ **cup chopped onion**
¼ **cup chopped green pepper**
3 **tablespoons dry red wine**
1 **clove garlic, minced**
1 **teaspoon dried oregano, crushed**
¼ **teaspoon salt**
 Dash pepper
1 **tablespoon cold water**
2 **teaspoons cornstarch**

Rinse chicken; pat dry. In a medium skillet combine *undrained* tomatoes, mushrooms, onion, green pepper, wine, garlic, oregano, salt, and pepper; place chicken atop vegetable mixture. Bring to boiling; reduce heat. Cover; simmer about 20 minutes or till chicken is tender and no longer pink. Transfer chicken to a serving platter; keep warm.

Stir together water and cornstarch; stir into skillet mixture. Cook and stir till thickened and bubbly. Cook and stir for 2 minutes more. Spoon sauce over chicken. Makes 4 servings. One serving equals:

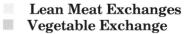 **Lean Meat Exchanges**
 Vegetable Exchange

ORANGE-SAUCED CHICKEN STIR-FRY

Tamari sauce is soy sauce made without wheat. Look for it in the Oriental section of your grocery store.

¾ **pound boned skinless chicken breast halves**
1 **cup unsweetened orange juice**
1 **tablespoon cornstarch**
1 **tablespoon dry sherry**
1 **tablespoon tamari *or* soy sauce**
½ **teaspoon ground ginger**
 Nonstick spray coating
4 **cups broccoli flowerets**
½ **cup sliced onion**
1 **tablespoon cooking oil**
1⅓ **cups hot cooked brown rice**
½ **of an orange, sliced**

Rinse chicken; pat dry. Cut the chicken into 1-inch pieces. Set aside. For sauce, stir together orange juice, cornstarch, sherry, tamari sauce, and ground ginger. Set aside.

Spray a *cold* wok or large skillet with nonstick coating. Preheat wok or skillet over medium heat. Add broccoli and onion; sir-fry for 2 to 3 minutes or till crisp-tender. Remove vegetables.

Add oil to wok or skillet. Then, add chicken; stir-fry for 2 to 4 minutes or till tender and no longer pink. Push chicken from center of wok or skillet.

Stir sauce; add to the center of the wok or skillet. Cook and stir till thickened and bubbly. Cook and stir for 2 minutes more. Return vegetables to wok or skillet; stir all ingredients together to coat with sauce. Serve immediately over rice. Garnish with orange slices. Makes 4 (1¼-cup) servings. One serving equals:

 Lean Meat Exchanges
 Starch/Bread Exchange
 Fruit Exchange
 Vegetable Exchanges
 Fat Exchange

CHEESE-STUFFED CHICKEN BREASTS

This baked chicken dish features two kinds of cheese—Parmesan on the outside, mozzarella on the inside.

4 **boned skinless chicken breast halves**
    (1 pound total)
4 **3x1x⅛-inch slices part-skim mozzarella**
    cheese (¾ ounce total)
1 **egg white**
2 **tablespoons all-purpose flour**
1 **tablespoon grated Parmesan cheese**
1 **teaspoon snipped parsley**
¼ **teaspoon paprika**
    Dash pepper
    Nonstick spray coating

Rinse chicken; pat dry. Use a sharp knife to cut a small pocket in the thickest side of each chicken breast half. Insert a mozzarella cheese slice in each pocket.

In a small mixing bowl beat egg white slightly. In another bowl stir together flour, Parmesan cheese, parsley, paprika, and pepper. Dip chicken in egg white. Then, coat with flour mixture.

Spray a 10x6x2-inch baking dish with nonstick coating. Arrange chicken in dish. Bake in a 375° oven for 20 to 25 minutes or till chicken is tender and no longer pink. Makes 4 servings. One serving equals:

■ ■ ■ ■ **Lean Meat Exchanges**

Cut a slit, just large enough to hold the cheese, in the meatiest side of each chicken breast half.

Tuck a slice of cheese into the pocket in each chicken breast half.

TEX-MEX TURKEY TENDERLOINS

A chunky sauce of chopped tomato, zucchini, and chili peppers tops spiced turkey steaks.

1 pound turkey tenderloin steaks,
    cut about ½ inch thick
1 teaspoon ground cumin
⅛ teaspoon salt
⅛ teaspoon pepper
   Nonstick spray coating
1 cup chopped seeded tomato
1 cup chopped zucchini
¼ cup sliced green onions
1 4-ounce can diced green chili peppers,
    drained
   Fresh chili peppers (optional)

Rinse turkey; pat dry. Stir together cumin, salt, and pepper; sprinkle on both sides of turkey tenderloin steaks.

Spray a *cold* large skillet with nonstick coating. Preheat over medium heat. Cook turkey in skillet for 10 to 12 minutes or till tender and no longer pink, turning once. Transfer turkey to serving platter. Cover with foil to keep warm.

Add tomato, zucchini, green onions, and diced chili peppers to skillet. Cook and stir over high heat for 1 to 2 minutes or till vegetables are crisp-tender. Spoon vegetable mixture over turkey. If desired, garnish with fresh chili peppers. Makes 4 servings. One serving equals:

    ■ ■ ■ **Lean Meat Exchanges**
        ■ **Vegetable Exchange**

LEMON CHICKEN WITH CURRIED RICE

If you like, serve the curried rice with other main dishes, such as broiled pork chops or fish fillets.

1 cup water
½ cup brown rice *or* long grain rice
2 tablespoons thinly sliced green onion
½ teaspoon curry powder
⅛ teaspoon salt
⅛ teaspoon ground ginger
4 boned skinless chicken breast halves
    (1 pound total)
   Nonstick spray coating
1 4-ounce can sliced mushrooms, drained
2 tablespoons water
1 tablespoon lemon juice
1 tablespoon reduced-sodium soy sauce
1 teaspoon snipped parsley

For curried rice, in a small saucepan combine 1 cup water, brown or long grain rice, green onion, curry powder, salt, and ginger. Bring to boiling; reduce heat. Cover and simmer about 40 minutes for brown rice (20 minutes for long grain rice) or till the liquid is absorbed.

Meanwhile, rinse chicken; pat dry. Place each breast half, boned side up, between two pieces of clear plastic wrap. Working from the center to the edges, pound the chicken lightly with the flat side of a meat mallet to ¼-inch thickness. Remove plastic wrap.

Spray a *cold* large skillet with nonstick coating. Preheat over medium heat. Cook chicken in skillet for 8 to 10 minutes or till tender and no longer pink, turning once. Remove from skillet; keep warm.

For sauce, add mushrooms, 2 tablespoons water, lemon juice, and soy sauce to skillet. Heat through, scraping up brown bits. Remove from heat. Spoon curried rice onto plates. Top with chicken. Ladle sauce over chicken and rice. Sprinkle with parsley. Makes 4 servings. One serving equals:

    ■ ■ ■ **Lean Meat Exchanges**
     ■ ■ **Starch/Bread Exchanges**

Tex-Mex
Turkey
Tenderloins

CHICKEN KABOBS WITH PEANUT SAUCE

To serve, dip tender strips of lime-marinated chicken breast in a creamy peanut butter and yogurt sauce.

¾ **pound boned skinless chicken breast halves**
¼ **cup reduced-sodium soy sauce**
2 **tablespoons lime *or* lemon juice**
½ **teaspoon garlic powder**
1 **cup green pepper cut into 1-inch pieces**
   Nonstick spray coating
¼ **cup skim milk**
1½ **teaspoons reduced-sodium soy sauce**
   Dash bottled hot pepper sauce
2 **tablespoons peanut butter**
½ **teaspoon cornstarch**
3 **tablespoons plain low-fat yogurt**

Rinse chicken; pat dry. Cut into ½-inch strips. Place chicken strips in a plastic bag set in a bowl. Set aside.

For marinade, stir together ¼ cup soy sauce, lime or lemon juice, and garlic powder. Pour over chicken; close bag. Refrigerate for 3 to 24 hours, turning bag occasionally.

Drain chicken strips, reserving marinade. On four 10- to 12-inch skewers, alternately thread chicken, accordion-style, and green pepper pieces. Spray the unheated rack of a broiler pan with nonstick coating. Place skewers on the rack. Broil 4 to 5 inches from the heat for 6 to 8 minutes or till chicken is tender and no longer pink, turning once and brushing frequently with marinade.

Meanwhile, for peanut sauce, combine milk, 1½ teaspoons soy sauce, and hot pepper sauce; set aside. In a small saucepan stir together peanut butter and cornstarch. Cook and stir over medium heat just till softened and mixed. Stir in yogurt and milk mixture. Cook and stir till thickened and bubbly. Cook and stir for 2 minutes more. Pass peanut sauce with chicken kabobs. Makes 4 servings. One serving equals:

▪ ▪ ▪ **Lean Meat Exchanges**
▪ **Fat Exchange**

ORIENTAL CHICKEN STIR-FRY

Oyster sauce lends a traditional Chinese flavor to this chicken and zucchini stir-fry.

½ **pound boned skinless chicken breast halves *or* turkey tenderloin steaks**
½ **cup water**
2 **tablespoons oyster sauce**
1 **tablespoon cornstarch**
1 **teaspoon soy sauce**
⅛ **teaspoon pepper**
   Nonstick spray coating
1 **clove garlic, minced**
1 **cup sliced zucchini**
½ **cup shredded carrot**
1 **teaspoon cooking oil**
½ **cup drained, canned bamboo shoots**
⅔ **cup hot cooked rice**

Rinse chicken or turkey; pat dry. Cut into thin bite-size pieces. Set aside. For sauce, stir together water, oyster sauce, cornstarch, soy sauce, and pepper. Set aside.

Spray a *cold* wok or large skillet with nonstick coating. Preheat over medium heat. Add garlic; stir-fry for 30 seconds. Add zucchini and carrot; stir-fry for 2 to 3 minutes or till vegetables are crisp-tender. Remove vegetable mixture; set aside.

Add oil to wok or skillet. Then, add chicken or turkey; stir-fry for 2 to 3 minutes or till tender and no longer pink. Push chicken or turkey from center of wok or skillet.

Stir the sauce; add to the center of the wok or skillet. Cook and stir till thickened and bubbly. Cook and stir for 2 minutes more. Add cooked vegetable mixture and bamboo shoots. Stir ingredients together to coat with sauce. Cook for 1 to 2 minutes more or till heated through. Serve with rice. Makes 2 (1¼-cup) servings. One serving equals:

▪ ▪ ▪ **Lean Meat Exchanges**
▪ **Starch/Bread Exchange**
▪ ▪ **Vegetable Exchanges**
▪ **Fat Exchange**

PLUM AND CHICKEN STIR-FRY

Plumb out of plums? Switch to fresh or frozen peaches.

¾ pound boned skinless chicken breast halves
⅓ cup water
2 tablespoons unsweetened orange juice
2 tablespoons rice wine vinegar *or* white wine vinegar
1 tablespoon soy sauce
2 teaspoons cornstarch
 Nonstick spray coating
1 small onion, thinly sliced and separated into rings
1 teaspoon cooking oil
1½ cups fresh plum slices, *or* sliced, peeled, fresh peaches, *or* frozen peach slices, thawed
1 6-ounce package frozen pea pods, thawed
1⅓ cups hot cooked rice

Rinse chicken; pat dry. Cut into thin bite-size strips. For marinade, stir together water, orange juice, vinegar, and soy sauce. Add chicken. Cover and let stand at room temperature for 30 minutes. Drain, reserving marinade. Stir cornstarch into marinade. Set aside.

Spray a *cold* wok or large skillet with nonstick coating. Preheat wok or skillet over medium heat. Add onion rings; stir-fry for 2 to 3 minutes or till tender; remove onion. Add oil to wok or skillet. Add chicken. Stir-fry for 2 to 3 minutes or till tender and no longer pink. Push chicken from center of the wok.

Stir marinade; add to center of wok or skillet. Cook and stir till thickened and bubbly. Cook and stir for 2 minutes more. Add plum or peach slices, pea pods, and cooked onion rings. Stir all ingredients together. Cook for 1 to 2 minutes more or till heated through. Serve with rice. Makes 4 (1¼-cup) servings. One serving equals:

 ■■ **Lean Meat Exchanges**
 ■ **Starch/Bread Exchange**
 ▮ **Fruit Exchange**
 ▮ **Vegetable Exchange**

WINE-MARINATED CHICKEN

For an elegant look, bias-slice each chicken breast half and arrange on a bed of rice or shredded lettuce.

⅓ cup dry white wine
½ teaspoon dried rosemary, crushed
¼ teaspoon salt
⅛ teaspoon garlic powder
⅛ teaspoon onion powder
⅛ teaspoon pepper
4 boned skinless chicken breast halves (1 pound total)
 Nonstick spray coating
 Paprika (optional)

For marinade, in a shallow dish combine wine, rosemary, salt, garlic powder, onion powder, and pepper.

Rinse chicken. Add chicken to marinade. Turn to coat chicken. Marinate for 30 minutes at room temperature or for 1 hour in the refrigerator.

Remove chicken from marinade, reserving marinade. Spray the unheated rack of a broiler pan with nonstick coating. Place chicken on the rack. Broil 4 to 5 inches from the heat for 6 minutes. Brush chicken with marinade. Turn and broil for 6 to 9 minutes more or till tender and no longer pink, basting often with the marinade. If desired, sprinkle with paprika. Makes 4 servings. One serving equals:

 ■■■ **Lean Meat Exchanges**

SWEET PEPPER AND TURKEY ROLLS

Give color to these turkey rolls by cutting strips from peppers of different colors. (Pictured on the cover.)

 1 small sweet red, green, *or* yellow pepper
 1 small zucchini
 6 turkey breast slices (¾ pound total)
    Nonstick spray coating
 3 tablespoons dry white wine
 2 tablespoons water
 2 tablespoons sliced green onion
 ½ teaspoon dried basil, crushed
 ¼ teaspoon salt
    Dash white pepper
 1 tablespoon cold water
1½ teaspoons cornstarch
 ½ teaspoon instant beef *or* chicken
    bouillon granules

Cut the pepper into thin strips. Trim ends from zucchini; cut in half crosswise. Cut each half into long thin strips. Divide pepper and zucchini strips among the turkey breast slices. Roll up turkey around vegetables. Secure with wooden toothpicks. Spray a 10x6x2-inch baking dish with nonstick coating. Arrange turkey rolls in dish.

Combine wine, 2 tablespoons water, green onion, basil, salt, and pepper. Pour over turkey rolls. Cover with foil. Bake in a 350° oven for 30 to 35 minutes or till the turkey is tender and no longer pink. Transfer turkey rolls to serving platter; keep warm.

For sauce, measure pan juices; add enough water to equal ½ cup liquid. In a small saucepan combine 1 tablespoon cold water, cornstarch, beef or chicken bouillon granules, and the pan juices. Cook and stir till thickened and bubbly. Cook and stir for 2 minutes more. Spoon sauce over turkey rolls. Makes 3 servings. One serving equals:

   ▪ ▪ ▪ **Lean Meat Exchanges**
     ▪ **Vegetable Exchange**

Roll the turkey slices around the vegetable strips. Use a wooden toothpick to hold the roll together.

TURKEY LOAF

 1 beaten egg white
 1 cup soft bread crumbs (1⅓ slices)
 ⅓ cup finely chopped onion
 ⅓ cup finely chopped green pepper
 2 tablespoons skim milk
 ½ teaspoon dried sage, crushed
 1 pound lean ground raw turkey
 2 tablespoons apricot all-fruit spread
 2 tablespoons catsup
 ½ teaspoon prepared mustard

In a mixing bowl combine egg white, bread crumbs, onion, green pepper, skim milk, sage, ¼ teaspoon *salt*, and ⅛ teaspoon *pepper*. Add turkey; mix well. In a shallow baking pan pat turkey mixture into a 6x4-inch loaf. Bake in a 350° oven for 45 minutes.

Meanwhile, for sauce, stir together apricot all-fruit spread, catsup, and mustard. Mix well. Drizzle over turkey loaf. Bake for 5 to 10 minutes more or till meat is no longer pink. Makes 4 servings. One serving equals:

   ▪ ▪ ▪ **Lean Meat Exchanges**
    ▮ **Starch/Bread Exchange**

TERIYAKI CHICKEN KABOBS

Round out your meal with hot cooked rice, steamed green beans, and fresh pineapple or melon.

1 cup sweet red *or* green pepper
    cut into 1-inch pieces
¼ cup water
¼ cup dry sherry
¼ cup reduced-sodium soy sauce
1 teaspoon grated gingerroot *or* ¼ teaspoon
    ground ginger
1 clove garlic, minced
¾ pound boned skinless chicken breast
    halves, cut into 1-inch pieces
6 large green onions, bias-sliced into
    1-inch lengths
    Nonstick spray coating

In a small saucepan cook red or green pepper in a small amount of boiling water for 2 minutes. Drain.

For marinade, in a mixing bowl stir together water, dry sherry, soy sauce, gingerroot or ginger, and garlic.

Set a plastic bag in a deep bowl; put chicken, green onion, and red or green pepper in the bag. Pour marinade over chicken mixture. Close bag. Marinate for 30 minutes at room temperature, turning bag once to coat all pieces. Drain; reserve marinade.

In a small saucepan bring reserved marinade to boiling; set aside. On four 10- to 12-inch skewers alternately thread chicken, green onion, and pepper. Spray the unheated rack of a broiler pan with nonstick coating. Place kabobs on the rack. Brush kabobs with marinade. Broil 4 inches from heat for 4 minutes. Turn; brush with marinade. Broil for 4 to 6 minutes more or till chicken is tender and no longer pink. Brush with marinade before serving. Makes 4 servings. One serving equals:

▪▪▪ **Lean Meat Exchanges**

GARLIC CHICKEN WITH PASTA

Simplify last-minute preparation by cutting up the chicken and vegetables the night before.

4 ounces corkscrew macaroni
¾ pound boned skinless chicken
    breast halves
⅔ cup chicken broth
2 teaspoons cornstarch
¼ teaspoon salt
¼ teaspoon pepper
    Nonstick spray coating
½ cup chopped onion
2 cloves garlic, minced
½ teaspoon dried oregano, crushed
¼ teaspoon dried thyme, crushed
1 cup sliced fresh mushrooms
1 cup halved zucchini slices
2 teaspoons cooking oil
½ cup chopped tomato

Cook pasta according to package directions, *except* omit oil. Drain well.

Meanwhile, rinse chicken; pat dry. Cut chicken into ¾-inch pieces. For sauce, stir together chicken broth, cornstarch, salt, and pepper; set aside.

Spray a *cold* wok or large skillet with nonstick coating. Preheat wok or skillet over medium heat. Add onion, garlic, oregano, and thyme; stir-fry for 2 minutes. Add mushrooms and zucchini; stir-fry for 2 to 3 minutes more or till vegetables are crisp-tender. Remove vegetables.

Add oil to wok or skillet. Then, add chicken; stir-fry for 3 to 4 minutes or till tender and no longer pink. Stir sauce; add to wok or skillet. Cook and stir till thickened and bubbly. Cook for 2 minutes more. Stir in tomato, vegetable mixture, and pasta. Cook till heated through. Makes 4 (1⅓-cup) servings. One serving equals:

▪▪▪ **Lean Meat Exchanges**
▪▪ **Starch/Bread Exchanges**
▪ **Vegetable Exchange**
▪ **Fat Exchange**

Turkey
Potpie

TURKEY POTPIE

So tasty and hearty you'll forget you're on a diet.

- 1 6-ounce can vegetable juice cocktail
- 4 teaspoons cornstarch
- 2 cups sliced small zucchini *and/or* yellow summer squash
- 1½ cups chopped tomatoes
- 1 tablespoon dried minced onion
- ½ teaspoon dried Italian seasoning, crushed
- ¼ teaspoon garlic powder
- ¼ teaspoon pepper
- 8 ounces cubed cooked turkey *or* chicken (1½ cups)
- ¾ cup packaged biscuit mix
- ¼ cup skim milk
- 1 tablespoon grated Parmesan cheese
- 1 teaspoon dried parsley flakes
  Fresh thyme sprigs (optional)
  Fresh oregano sprigs (optional)

In a small mixing bowl stir together *2 table-spoons* of the vegetable juice cocktail and cornstarch; set aside.

In a large saucepan mix zucchini and/or summer squash, tomatoes, onion, Italian seasoning, garlic powder, pepper, and remaining vegetable juice cocktail. Bring to boiling. Add turkey or chicken and cornstarch mixture. Cook and stir till thickened and bubbly. Reduce heat and keep warm.

For biscuit topping, in a medium mixing bowl stir together biscuit mix, milk, Parmesan cheese, and parsley just till moistened.

Transfer the hot chicken mixture to a 1½-quart casserole. Immediately, drop biscuit topping in 4 mounds atop chicken mixture. Place casserole on a baking sheet.

Bake in a 400° oven for 15 to 20 minutes or till the topping is golden. If desired, garnish with fresh thyme and oregano. Makes 4 (1⅓-cup) servings. One serving equals:

▫ ▫ **Lean Meat Exchanges**
■   **Starch/Bread Exchange**
▪   **Vegetable Exchange**
■   **Fat Exchange**

TURKEY HAM PILAF

This tasty off-the-shelf recipe makes a one-dish meal.

- 1¼ cups water
- 1 cup quick-cooking brown rice
- ½ teaspoon onion powder
- ½ teaspoon instant chicken bouillon granules
- ¼ teaspoon pepper
- ⅛ teaspoon garlic powder
- 1 10-ounce package frozen cut asparagus *or* cut broccoli, *or* one 9-ounce package frozen French-style green beans
- 1 tablespoon white wine vinegar
- 1 tablespoon dry sherry *or* dry white wine
- 6 ounces fully cooked turkey ham *or* fully cooked ham, cut into bite-size strips
- 2 tablespoons sliced almonds, toasted

In a large saucepan combine water, rice, onion powder, bouillon granules, pepper, and garlic powder. Bring to boiling; reduce heat. Cover and simmer for 12 to 14 minutes or till all the liquid is absorbed.

Meanwhile, cook frozen vegetables according to package directions; drain.

Stir vinegar and sherry or wine into rice mixture; mix well. Stir in turkey ham or ham, almonds, and cooked vegetables; heat through. Makes 4 (1-cup) servings. One serving equals:

▫   **Lean Meat Exchange**
■ ■ ■ **Starch/Bread Exchanges**
▫   **Vegetable Exchange**
▪   **Fat Exchange**

33

MANDARIN CHICKEN DINNER

Millet, which you can buy in health food stores, provides the starch/bread exchange in this one-dish meal.

1¼ cups water
1 cup sliced celery
½ cup millet
¼ cup sliced green onions
1½ cups chopped cooked chicken (8 ounces)
1 8-ounce can sliced water chestnuts, drained
2 tablespoons soy sauce
1 10½-ounce can mandarin orange sections (water pack), drained

In a large saucepan combine water, celery, millet, and green onions. Bring to boiling; reduce heat. Cover and simmer for 10 to 15 minutes or till liquid is absorbed.

Stir chicken, water chestnuts, and soy sauce into the millet mixture; heat through. Gently fold in orange sections. Makes 4 (1½-cup) servings. One serving equals:

▪▪ Lean Meat Exchanges
▪▪ Starch/Bread Exchanges
▪▪ Vegetable Exchanges

TACO CHICKEN STEW

Save yourself some time and purchase frozen diced cooked chicken for this spicy stew.

1 28-ounce can tomatoes, cut up
1 15-ounce can pinto beans, drained
1 4-ounce can diced green chili peppers, drained
¼ cup chopped onion
2 teaspoons instant chicken bouillon granules
⅛ teaspoon garlic powder
⅛ teaspoon ground cumin
1½ cups chopped cooked chicken (8 ounces)

In a large saucepan combine *undrained* tomatoes, beans, chili peppers, onion, bouillon granules, garlic powder, cumin, and 1½ cups *water*. Bring to boiling; reduce heat. Cover and simmer for 10 minutes. Stir in chicken; heat through. Makes 4 (1½-cup) servings. One serving equals:

▪▪ Lean Meat Exchanges
▪▪ Starch/Bread Exchanges
▪▪ Vegetable Exchanges

SMOKED TURKEY SALAD

Fresh dill perks up the flavor of bottled salad dressing.

3 cups shredded lettuce
1 cup chopped tomato
1 cup thinly sliced cucumber
4 ounces fully cooked smoked turkey breast, cut into julienne strips
¼ cup bias-sliced celery
¼ cup reduced-calorie blue cheese salad dressing
1 teaspoon snipped fresh dill *or* ¼ teaspoon dried dillweed

Line two salad plates with lettuce. Top with tomato and cucumber. Then, arrange turkey strips and celery on the plates. Stir together salad dressing and dill; drizzle over salad. Makes 2 servings. One serving equals:

▪▪ Lean Meat Exchanges
▪ Vegetable Exchange
▪ Fat Exchange

TURKEY WALDORF SALAD

Before shredding the cabbage, carefully remove two cabbage leaves to use as serving bowls.

2 cups shredded cabbage
1 cup chopped cooked turkey (5 ounces)
1 cup chopped apple
½ cup halved seedless red *or* green grapes
¼ cup sliced celery
¼ cup reduced-calorie buttermilk *or* creamy cucumber salad dressing
2 tablespoons skim milk
2 cabbage leaves

In a medium mixing bowl combine shredded cabbage, turkey, apple, grapes, and celery.

In a small mixing bowl combine salad dressing and milk. Pour over turkey mixture and toss. (If desired, place in freezer for 20 minutes to quick-chill.)

For each serving, spoon half of the turkey mixture into a cabbage leaf. Makes 2 (2-cup) servings. One serving equals:

◻◻ **Lean Meat Exchanges**
◼ **Fruit Exchange**
◻ **Vegetable Exchange**
▮◼ **Fat Exchanges**

FRUITED CHICKEN SALAD

A creamy apricot dressing generously coats chicken chunks, grape halves, and orange sections.

1 4½-ounce jar strained apricot with tapioca baby food
¼ cup plain low-fat yogurt
2 tablespoons skim milk
1½ cups chopped cooked chicken (8 ounces)
1 cup thinly sliced celery
½ cup halved red *or* green seedless grapes
2 tablespoons thinly sliced green onion
1 10½-ounce can mandarin orange sections (water pack), drained

Mix baby food, yogurt, milk, ½ teaspoon *salt*, and ⅛ teaspoon *pepper*. Stir in chicken, celery, grapes, and onion. Cover; chill 2 to 24 hours. To serve, stir in oranges. Makes 4 (1-cup) servings. One serving equals:

◻◻ **Lean Meat Exchanges**
▮ **Fruit Exchange**

MICRO-COOKING POULTRY

When you need cooked chicken or turkey for a recipe in short order, your microwave oven can fill the bill. Here's how:

For 1¼ cups chopped, cooked poultry, place 8 ounces boned skinless chicken breast halves or turkey breast tenderloin steaks in a 10x6x2-inch microwave-safe baking dish. Cover with vented microwave-safe plastic wrap. Micro-cook on 100% power (high) for 1½ minutes. Turn pieces over and rearrange in dish by moving the outside pieces to center of dish. Cook, covered, on high for 1 to 2 minutes more or till meat is tender and no longer pink. Cool and cut up.

GARLIC-MARINATED SWORDFISH STEAKS

Swordfish and halibut each have a firm texture that makes them easy to broil.

1   pound fresh *or* frozen swordfish *or*
     halibut steaks
¼   cup unsweetened pineapple *or*
     orange juice
2   tablespoons finely chopped green onion
1   tablespoon cooking oil
1   tablespoon reduced-sodium soy sauce
1   clove garlic, minced
½   teaspoon grated gingerroot
     Nonstick spray coating

Thaw fish steaks, if frozen. Cut into 4 serving-size portions.

For marinade, in a shallow dish combine pineapple or orange juice, green onion, oil, soy sauce, garlic, and grated gingerroot. Add fish steaks; turn to coat. Cover and marinate in the refrigerator for 4 to 6 hours, turning fish occasionally.

Drain fish, reserving marinade. Measure thickness of fish. Spray unheated rack of a broiler pan with nonstick coating. Place fish on the rack. Broil 4 inches from the heat till fish just flakes with a fork, brushing occasionally with reserved marinade. Allow 4 to 6 minutes for each ½-inch thickness of fish. (If your fish steaks are more than 1 inch thick, turn them over halfway through broiling.) Makes 4 servings. One serving equals:

     Lean Meat Exchanges
▪ **Fat Exchange**

FLOUNDER DIJON

A creamy vegetable-mustard sauce tops mild-tasting flounder fillets for an easy, yet elegant entrée.

4   3-ounce fresh *or* frozen flounder,
     sole, *or* pompano fillets
     Nonstick spray coating
½   cup sliced fresh mushrooms
⅓   cup sliced zucchini
¼   cup julienne carrot strips (1-inch pieces)
¼   cup sliced green onion
¾   cup skim milk
1½ teaspoons cornstarch
1½ teaspoons Dijon-style mustard
1   teaspoon instant chicken bouillon
     granules

Thaw fish, if frozen. Measure thickness of fish. Place the fish in a single layer in a 12x7½x2-inch baking dish; tuck under any thin edges. Bake in a 450° oven till fish just flakes with a fork. Allow 4 to 6 minutes for each ½-inch thickness of fish.

Meanwhile, for the sauce, spray a *cold* medium saucepan with nonstick coating. Preheat saucepan over medium heat. Cook mushrooms, zucchini, carrot, and green onion in saucepan till crisp-tender. Stir together skim milk, cornstarch, Dijon-style mustard, and chicken bouillon granules. Add milk mixture to vegetables in saucepan. Cook and stir till thickened and bubbly. Cook and stir for 2 minutes more. Transfer fish to dinner plates. Ladle sauce over fish. Makes 4 servings. One serving equals:

     Lean Meat Exchanges
  Vegetable Exchange

Flounder
Dijon

OVEN-FRIED FISH

Orange peel and soy sauce give an exotic taste to this crumb-coated fish.

1 **pound fresh *or* frozen skinless fish fillets**
  Nonstick spray coating
1 **tablespoon reduced-sodium soy sauce**
¼ **cup fine dry bread crumbs**
2 **teaspoons margarine *or* butter, melted**
1 **teaspoon finely shredded orange peel**

Thaw fish, if frozen. If necessary, cut the fish into 4 serving-size portions. Measure thickness of fish.

Spray a 12x7½x2-inch baking dish with nonstick coating. Place fish in a single layer in the dish, tucking under any thin edges.

Brush fish with soy sauce. In a small mixing bowl stir together bread crumbs, margarine or butter, and orange peel. Sprinkle crumb mixture on top of fish. Bake in a 450° oven till fish just flakes with a fork. Allow 4 to 6 minutes for each ½-inch thickness of fish. Makes 4 servings. One serving equals:

    Lean Meat Exchanges
▮ **Starch/Bread Exchange**
▮ **Fat Exchange**

MEXICAN-STYLE FISH FILLETS

Simmer fish fillets in a peppy fresh tomato sauce for a slimming south-of-the-border meal.

1 **pound fresh *or* frozen red snapper, orange roughy, *or* other fish fillets**
1½ **cups chopped, seeded, peeled tomatoes**
¼ **cup sliced green onions**
¼ **cup water**
1 **clove garlic, minced**
1½ **teaspoons chili powder**
1 **teaspoon instant chicken bouillon granules**
  Dash bottled hot pepper sauce (optional)
2 **tablespoons water**
4 **teaspoons cornstarch**
1⅓ **cups hot cooked rice**
4 **lime wedges**

Thaw fish, if frozen. If necessary, cut fish fillets into 4 serving-size portions. Measure thickness of fish.

In a large skillet combine tomatoes, green onions, ¼ cup water, garlic, chili powder, chicken bouillon granules, and, if desired, bottled hot pepper sauce. Bring to boiling; reduce heat. Cover and simmer mixture for 5 minutes.

Carefully add fish. Return to boiling; reduce heat. Cover and simmer till fish just flakes with a fork. Allow 4 to 6 minutes for each ½-inch thickness of fish. Transfer fish to a serving platter; keep warm.

For sauce, stir together 2 tablespoons water and cornstarch. Add to tomato mixture in skillet. Cook and stir till thickened and bubbly. Cook and stir for 2 minutes more. Ladle sauce over fish on platter. Serve fish with rice and lime wedges. Makes 4 servings. One serving equals:

    Lean Meat Exchanges
▮ **Vegetable Exchange**
▮ **Starch/Bread Exchange**

ORIENTAL FISH WITH PASTA

This teriyaki-flavored stir-fry is served over linguine.

¾ pound fresh *or* frozen tuna, swordfish, *or* halibut steaks, cut ¾ inch thick
¾ pound asparagus spears
¼ cup dry white wine
2 tablespoons teriyaki sauce
1 tablespoon water
2 teaspoons cornstarch
¼ teaspoon five-spice powder *(see tip, page 54)*
   Nonstick spray coating
1 clove garlic, minced
1 tablespoon cooking oil
⅔ cup halved cherry tomatoes
½ of an 8-ounce can (½ cup) sliced water chestnuts, drained
2 cups hot cooked linguine

Thaw fish, if frozen. Cut into ¾-inch cubes. Remove tough portion of each asparagus stem. Bias-slice asparagus into 1-inch lengths. For sauce, stir together white wine, teriyaki sauce, water, cornstarch, and five-spice powder. Set aside.

Spray a *cold* wok or large skillet with nonstick coating. Preheat wok or skillet over medium heat. Add garlic; stir-fry for 15 seconds. Add asparagus; stir-fry for 4 to 5 minutes or till crisp-tender. Remove asparagus.

Add oil to wok or skillet. Add fish; stir-fry for 3 to 5 minutes or till fish just flakes with a fork. Push fish from center of wok.

Stir sauce; add to center of wok or skillet. Cook and stir till thickened and bubbly. Cook and stir for 2 minutes more. Return asparagus to wok or skillet. Add cherry tomatoes and water chestnuts; stir all ingredients together. Cover and cook for 1 minute or till heated through. Ladle fish mixture over linguine. Makes 4 (1½-cup) servings. One serving equals:

- ▪ ▪ **Lean Meat Exchanges**
- ▪ **Starch/Bread Exchange**
- ▪ ▪ **Vegetable Exchanges**
- ▪ **Fat Exchange**

LEMON-POACHED HALIBUT

A chilled carrot-and-mayonnaise sauce accompanies the fish steaks.

1 pound fresh *or* frozen halibut *or* other fish steaks
½ cup reduced-calorie mayonnaise *or* salad dressing
¼ cup finely shredded carrot
1 tablespoon finely chopped dill pickle
1 teaspoon finely chopped onion
1 teaspoon snipped parsley
1 teaspoon lemon juice
3 cups water
⅓ cup sliced onion
⅛ cup lemon juice
¼ cup chopped celery
¼ teaspoon salt
⅛ teaspoon pepper
4 lemon wedges

Thaw fish, if frozen. Cut fish into 4 serving-size portions. Measure thickness of fish.

Meanwhile, for sauce, stir together mayonnaise or salad dressing, carrot, dill pickle, chopped onion, parsley, and 1 teaspoon lemon juice. Cover and chill thoroughly.

In a large skillet combine water, sliced onion, ⅓ cup lemon juice, celery, salt, and pepper. Bring to boiling; reduce heat. Simmer, uncovered, for 5 minutes. Carefully add fish. Return to boiling; reduce heat. Cover and simmer till fish just flakes with a fork. Allow 4 to 6 minutes for each ½-inch thickness of fish. Remove fish from liquid. Serve with chilled sauce and lemon wedges. *Or,* chill fish for 2 to 24 hours before serving. Makes 4 servings. One serving equals:

- ▪ ▪ ▪ **Lean Meat Exchanges**
- ▪ **Vegetable Exchange**
- ▪ ▪ **Fat Exchanges**

CHILLED POACHED FISH

The refreshingly cold fish fillet is complemented by a flavor-packed horseradish sauce.

¾ pound fresh *or* frozen cod, flounder, or-
    ange roughy, *or* other skinless fish fillets
1 lemon, sliced
⅔ cup plain low-fat yogurt
¼ cup finely chopped, seeded, peeled tomato
1 tablespoon sliced green onion
1 teaspoon snipped fresh cilantro *or* parsley
½ teaspoon prepared horseradish
¼ teaspoon salt
¼ teaspoon lime *or* lemon juice
¼ teaspoon Dijon-style mustard
⅛ teaspoon paprika
2 cups shredded lettuce

Thaw fish, if frozen. Cut into 4 serving-size portions. Measure thickness of fish.

In a large skillet bring 1½ cups *water* to boiling. Carefully add fish and lemon. Return to boiling; reduce heat. Cover and simmer till fish just flakes with a fork. Allow 4 to 6 minutes for each ½-inch thickness of fish. Using a large slotted spatula, remove fish from skillet. Carefully immerse fish in a bowl of ice water for 1 to 2 minutes or till thoroughly chilled. Remove fish from ice water; chill fish for 2 to 24 hours.

For sauce, stir together yogurt, chopped tomato, sliced green onion, cilantro or parsley, horseradish, salt, lime or lemon juice, mustard, and paprika. Cover and chill at least 2 hours. To serve, place chilled fish on lettuce-lined plates. Serve with sauce. Makes 4 servings. One serving equals:

    ■ ■ **Lean Meat Exchanges**
    ■ **Milk Exchange**

EASY BAKED FISH

Start with a convenient package of frozen fish portions.

1 11½-ounce package (4 portions) frozen
    fish portions
¼ teaspoon lemon pepper
¼ teaspoon dried basil, crushed
1 small tomato, cut into 4 slices
2 tablespoons sliced green onions
2 tablespoons grated Parmesan cheese

In an 8x8x2-inch baking dish arrange frozen fish portions. Sprinkle with lemon pepper and basil.

Bake in a 375° oven for 15 minutes. Place a tomato slice on each fish portion. Sprinkle with green onions and Parmesan cheese. Bake about 10 minutes more or till fish just flakes with a fork. Makes 4 servings. One serving equals:

    ■ ■ **Lean Meat Exchanges**
    ■ **Vegetable Exchange**

To chill the poached fish and stop further cooking, lower fillets, one at a time, into a bowl of ice water.

SPINACH-TOPPED HALIBUT

Creamed spinach becomes a tasty sauce when ladled over fish steaks.

 1 pound fresh *or* frozen halibut *or*
   cod steaks
 2 cups water
 ¼ cup lemon juice
 ¼ teaspoon salt
 ½ of a 10-ounce package frozen
   chopped spinach
 ¼ cup chopped onion
 ¼ cup chopped celery
 ¾ cup skim milk
 1 tablespoon cornstarch
 ⅛ teaspoon ground nutmeg
 ⅛ teaspoon pepper
 2 tablespoons grated Parmesan cheese

Thaw fish, if frozen. If necessary, cut into 4 serving-size portions. Measure the thickness of the fish.

In a large skillet combine water, lemon juice, and salt. Bring to boiling. Carefully add fish. Return to boiling; reduce heat. Cover and simmer till fish just flakes with a fork. Allow 4 to 6 minutes for each ½-inch thickness of fish. Transfer fish to a platter; keep warm.

Meanwhile, in a medium saucepan cook spinach, onion, and celery, covered, in a small amount of boiling water for 5 minutes. Drain spinach mixture in a colander, pressing out excess liquid.

In the same saucepan combine milk, cornstarch, nutmeg, and pepper. Cook and stir till thickened and bubbly. Cook and stir for 2 minutes more. Stir in spinach mixture; heat through. Spoon ¼ cup of the spinach mixture over each fish portion. Sprinkle with Parmesan cheese. Makes 4 servings. One serving equals:

    ▪ ▪ ▪ **Lean Meat Exchanges**
       ▪ **Vegetable Exchange**

POACHED FISH WITH LIME SAUCE

Drape the velvety smooth yogurt sauce over the fish steaks and, if you like, garnish with a lime slice.

 1 pound fresh *or* frozen halibut, cod, *or*
   other fish steaks
 1 cup water
 2 tablespoons sliced green onions
 ¼ teaspoon finely shredded lime peel
 2 tablespoons lime juice
 ¼ teaspoon salt
 ¼ teaspoon dried rosemary, crushed
 ⅛ teaspoon pepper
 ½ cup plain low-fat yogurt
 1 tablespoon cornstarch

Thaw fish, if frozen. Cut into 4 serving-size portions. Measure thickness of fish.

In a large skillet combine water, green onions, lime peel, lime juice, salt, rosemary, and pepper. Bring to boiling. Carefully add fish. Return to boiling; reduce heat. Cover and simmer till fish just flakes with a fork. Allow 4 to 6 minutes for each ½-inch thickness of fish. Using a large slotted spatula, transfer fish to a serving platter, leaving cooking liquid in skillet. Keep fish warm.

For sauce, bring liquid in skillet to boiling. Boil about 1 minute or till reduced to ⅔ *cup.* Stir together yogurt and cornstarch; add to cooking liquid. Cook and stir till thickened and bubbly. Cook and stir for 2 minutes more. Ladle sauce over the fish. Makes 4 servings. One serving equals:

    ▪ ▪ ▪ **Lean Meat Exchanges**

Fruited Crab Salad

FRUITED CRAB SALAD

Be sure to use real crabmeat. Frozen crab-flavored fish products contain sugar.

1 8-ounce can unpeeled apricot
    halves (water pack), drained
1 6-ounce package frozen crabmeat,
    thawed and drained
1 cup sliced strawberries
¾ cup sliced celery
¼ cup reduced-calorie mayonnaise
    or salad dressing
¼ cup plain low-fat yogurt
1 to 2 tablespoons skim milk
½ teaspoon curry powder
4 cups torn salad greens

Cut apricot pieces in half. In a large mixing bowl combine apricots, crabmeat, strawberries, and celery.

For dressing, in a small mixing bowl stir together mayonnaise or salad dressing, plain low-fat yogurt, milk, and curry powder. Line three salad plates with torn salad greens. Arrange *one-third* of the crab mixture on *each* plate. Drizzle with dressing. Makes 3 (1⅓-cup) servings. One serving equals:

   Lean Meat Exchange
▪ Fruit Exchange
   Vegetable Exchange
▪ Fat Exchange

STIR-FRIED SCALLOPS WITH PASTA

Capellini is a very fine, long pasta that's also called angel-hair pasta.

1 pound fresh *or* frozen bay scallops
4 ounces capellini, linguine, *or* other pasta
¼ cup dry white wine
2 tablespoons water
2 teaspoons cornstarch
½ teaspoon instant chicken bouillon
    granules
2 cloves garlic, minced
1 tablespoon margarine *or* butter
1½ cups sliced fresh mushrooms
½ cup sliced green onions
½ cup shredded carrot
1 tablespoon snipped parsley
4 lemon wedges

Thaw scallops, if frozen. Cook pasta according to package directions, *except* omit oil; drain and keep warm.

Meanwhile, for sauce, stir together wine, water, cornstarch, and chicken bouillon granules; set aside.

In a large skillet cook garlic in hot margarine or butter for 30 seconds. Add mushrooms, green onions, and carrot; stir-fry for 2 to 3 minutes or till carrot is crisp-tender.

Stir sauce. Add sauce, scallops, and snipped parsley to vegetable mixture in skillet. Cook and stir till the sauce is thickened and bubbly. Cook and stir for 2 minutes more or till the scallops are opaque. Serve with pasta and lemon wedges. Makes 4 (1¼-cup) servings. One serving equals:

      Lean Meat Exchanges
▪ ▪ Starch/Bread Exchanges
      Vegetable Exchange
▪ Fat Exchange

SAUCY SHRIMP WITH ARTICHOKE HEARTS

Dijon mustard and white wine lend a gourmet flavor to the sauce in this elegant dinner dish.

 1 9-ounce package frozen artichoke hearts
 1 pound fresh *or* frozen peeled and deveined shrimp
 5 teaspoons cornstarch
 1 teaspoon instant chicken bouillon granules
 ⅛ teaspoon pepper
 1¼ cups skim milk
 1 tablespoon Dijon-style mustard
 ¼ cup dry white wine
 1⅓ cups hot cooked rice

In a large saucepan bring 3 cups *water* to boiling. Add artichoke hearts. Return to boiling; reduce heat. Cover and simmer for 5 minutes. Add fresh or frozen shrimp. Return to boiling. Reduce heat. Simmer, uncovered, for 3 to 4 minutes or till shrimp turn pink. Drain artichoke hearts and shrimp; return to saucepan and set aside.

Meanwhile, for sauce, in a medium saucepan stir together cornstarch, chicken bouillon granules, and pepper. Gradually stir in skim milk and mustard. Cook and stir till mixture is thickened and bubbly. Cook and stir for 2 minutes more. Stir in wine.

Gently stir sauce into shrimp mixture in the other saucepan. Heat through. Ladle shrimp mixture over hot cooked rice. Makes 6 (1-cup) servings. One serving equals:

 ▪ Lean Meat Exchange
 ▪ Starch/Bread Exchange
 ▪ Vegetable Exchange

POLYNESIAN SHRIMP

You may substitute 3 cups of fresh pea pods for the frozen ones; add them with the green onions.

 12 ounces fresh *or* frozen peeled and deveined medium *or* large shrimp
 1½ cups bias-sliced carrots (½-inch pieces)
 1 cup unsweetened pineapple juice
 2 tablespoons soy sauce
 1 tablespoon cornstarch
    Nonstick spray coating
 2 teaspoons grated gingerroot
 1 clove garlic, minced
 ¼ cup bias-sliced green onions (½-inch pieces)
 1 tablespoon cooking oil
 1 6-ounce package frozen pea pods, thawed
 1⅓ cups hot cooked rice

Thaw shrimp, if frozen. If using large shrimp, cut lengthwise in half. Set aside. In a small saucepan cook carrots, covered, in a small amount of boiling salted water for 3 minutes; drain and set aside. For sauce, stir together pineapple juice, soy sauce, and cornstarch; set aside.

Spray a *cold* wok or large skillet with nonstick coating. Preheat wok or skillet over medium heat. Add gingerroot and garlic; stir-fry for ½ minute. Add carrots and green onions; stir-fry about 1 minute or till heated through. Remove vegetable mixture.

Add oil to wok or skillet. Then, add shrimp; stir-fry for 2 to 3 minutes or till shrimp turn pink. Push shrimp from center of wok.

Stir sauce; add to center of wok or skillet. Cook and stir till thickened and bubbly. Cook and stir for 2 minutes more. Return vegetable mixture to wok. Add pea pods. Stir all ingredients together to coat with sauce. Cover and cook for 1 minute or till heated through. Serve over hot cooked rice. Makes 4 (1⅓-cup) servings. One serving equals:

 ▪ ▪ Lean Meat Exchanges
 ▪ Starch/Bread Exchange
 ▪ Fruit Exchange
 ▪ Vegetable Exchange
 ▪ Fat Exchange

HEARTY SALMON PIE

This potato-topped casserole makes an excellent choice for low-calorie, family-style dining.

Packaged instant mashed potatoes
  (enough for 4 servings)
½ **cup shredded carrot**
¼ **cup finely chopped sweet red** *or*
  green pepper
¼ **cup finely chopped celery**
1 **slightly beaten egg**
2 **cups soft bread crumbs (2½ slices bread)**
⅓ **cup skim milk**
1 **tablespoon margarine** *or* **butter, melted**
½ **teaspoon dried Italian seasoning, crushed**
¼ **teaspoon onion powder**
1 **15½-ounce can salmon, drained, flaked,**
  and skin and bones removed
  Nonstick spray coating
2 **tablespoons snipped chives**

Prepare instant mashed potatoes according to package directions, *except* omit margarine or butter and use *skim* milk; set aside.

In a small saucepan cook carrot, sweet red or green pepper, and celery, covered, in a small amount of boiling water for 2 to 3 minutes or till crisp-tender. Drain; set aside.

In a medium mixing bowl combine egg, bread crumbs, milk, margarine or butter, Italian seasoning, onion powder, and cooked carrot mixture. Stir in salmon; mix well.

Spray a 9-inch pie plate with nonstick coating. Spread salmon mixture in pie plate. Dollop mashed potatoes around edge. Bake in a 350° oven about 30 minutes or till salmon mixture is set and potatoes start to brown. Let stand 5 minutes. Sprinkle potatoes with chives. Cut into wedges to serve. Makes 6 servings. One serving equals:

  Lean Meat Exchanges
  Starch/Bread Exchanges
  Vegetable Exchange
  Fat Exchange

TANGY SALMON SALAD

For a sandwich, spoon the salad into a pita half. Then, remember to add a Bread Exchange to your daily tally.

½ **cup sliced celery**
¼ **cup reduced-calorie mayonnaise** *or*
  salad dressing
2 **tablespoons sliced green onions**
2 **tablespoons dill relish**
1 **tablespoon lemon juice**
  Dash pepper
1 **7¾-ounce can salmon, drained, flaked,**
  and skin and bones removed
2 **cups shredded lettuce**

In a medium mixing bowl combine celery, mayonnaise or salad dressing, green onions, relish, lemon juice, and pepper; mix well. Add salmon; toss to coat. Cover and chill till serving time. To serve, spoon salmon mixture onto lettuce-lined plates. Makes 2 (1¾-cup) servings. One serving equals:

  Lean Meat Exchanges
  Vegetable Exchange
  Fat Exchanges

TUNA TOSS

You get a large serving because this salad includes free foods—salad greens, celery, and cucumber.

4 **cups torn salad greens**
¾ **cup halved cherry tomatoes**
½ **cup sliced cucumber**
1 **small onion, thinly sliced and separated**
  into rings
¼ **cup sliced celery**
1 **6½-ounce can tuna (water pack), drained**
  and broken into chunks
⅓ **cup bottled oil-free Italian salad dressing**

In a large salad bowl combine greens, tomatoes, cucumber, onion, and celery. Add tuna and salad dressing. Toss lightly till all the ingredients are coated with dressing. Makes 4 (1½-cup) servings. One serving equals:

  Lean Meat Exchanges
  Vegetable Exchange
  Fat Exchange

TUNA BULGUR SALAD

Tote this salad to the office for lunch. Just pack it in an insulated container and enjoy within 4 hours.

½ cup bulgur
1 cup chopped, seeded cucumber
¼ cup snipped parsley
¼ cup water
2 tablespoons sliced green onions
2 tablespoons lemon juice
4 teaspoons salad oil
½ teaspoon garlic salt
1 cup chopped, seeded tomato
1 6½-ounce can tuna (water pack), drained and broken into chunks
Lettuce leaves

Place bulgur in a colander. Rinse with cold water. Drain well.

In a medium mixing bowl combine the drained bulgur, cucumber, parsley, water, green onions, lemon juice, salad oil, and garlic salt. Mix well. Stir in tomato and tuna; toss to mix. Cover and chill overnight. Makes 4 (1-cup) servings. One serving equals:

    ■ **Lean Meat Exchange**
    ■ **Starch/Bread Exchange**
    ■ **Vegetable Exchange**
    ■ **Fat Exchange**

TUNA POCKETS

A quartet of vegetables makes this a colorful, crunchy, and fresh-tasting tuna sandwich filling.

1 6½-ounce can tuna (water pack), drained and broken into chunks
1 cup chopped, seeded cucumber
½ cup chopped, seeded tomato
½ cup shredded carrot
¼ cup reduced-calorie creamy Italian salad dressing *or* other reduced-calorie creamy salad dressing
2 6-inch pita bread rounds
½ cup alfalfa sprouts

In a medium mixing bowl combine tuna, cucumber, tomato, and carrot. Add salad dressing; toss lightly to coat. Cover and chill at least 1 hour.

Cut pitas in half crosswise. Carefully open pockets. Divide tuna mixture among the pita halves. Top each with alfalfa sprouts. Makes 4 servings. One serving equals:

    ■ **Lean Meat Exchanges**
    ■ **Starch/Bread Exchange**
    ■ **Vegetable Exchange**

CHOOSING A SALAD DRESSING

In a muddle over which salad dressing to buy? Use the nutrition information on the label as your guide. Up to 2 tablespoons of a low-calorie salad dressing containing less than 10 calories per tablespoon is a Free Exchange. For a reduced-calorie salad dressing (less than 45 calories per tablespoon), count 2 tablespoons as 1 Fat Exchange. Choose regular salad dressings less often, since you are allowed only 1 tablespoon of dressing for 1 Fat Exchange.

Tuna
Pockets

ROAST BEEF WITH MUSHROOM SAUCE

By using an eye of round roast, you're starting with meat that's naturally lean.

1   2-pound beef eye of round roast
½   teaspoon dried marjoram, crushed
¼   teaspoon salt
¼   teaspoon pepper
1   cup water
¼   cup dry red wine
1   tablespoon cornstarch
1½ teaspoons instant beef bouillon granules
1   teaspoon Worcestershire sauce
⅛   teaspoon dried marjoram, crushed
1   4-ounce can sliced mushrooms, drained
1   tablespoon snipped parsley

Trim separable fat from roast. Place roast on a rack in a shallow roasting pan. In a small bowl combine the ½ teaspoon marjoram, salt, and pepper. Rub over roast. Insert a meat thermometer into the roast.

For medium doneness, roast in a 325° oven for 1¾ to 2¼ hours or till meat thermometer registers 160°. Remove meat from the oven. Let stand for 15 minutes.

Meanwhile, for sauce, in a small saucepan stir together the water, wine, cornstarch, bouillon granules, Worcestershire, and the ⅛ teaspoon marjoram. Cook and stir till thickened and bubbly. Cook and stir 2 minutes more. Stir in mushrooms; heat through. Carve roast, by bias-slicing across the grain. Serve sauce with meat. Sprinkle with parsley. Makes 8 servings. One serving equals:

■ ■ ■   **Lean Meat Exchanges**

OLD-FASHIONED BEEF STEW

Robust, rich flavors and bright colors create a feast for your senses.

¾   pound boneless beef round steak
    Nonstick spray coating
1   14½-ounce can beef broth
2   bay leaves
2   cloves garlic, minced
1   tablespoon Worcestershire sauce
½   teaspoon paprika
⅛   teaspoon pepper
    Dash ground cloves
3   cups potatoes cut into 1-inch pieces
1½ cups carrots cut into 1-inch pieces
1   medium onion, cut into 8 wedges
¼   cup cold water
2   teaspoons cornstarch

Trim separable fat from steak. Cut into 1-inch cubes. Spray a *cold* Dutch oven with nonstick coating. Preheat over medium heat. Add the beef to the hot Dutch oven; cook till brown. Stir in broth, bay leaves, garlic, Worcestershire sauce, paprika, pepper, and cloves. Bring to boiling; reduce heat. Cover; simmer for 1 to 1¼ hours or till meat is almost tender, stirring occasionally. Remove bay leaves. Stir in potatoes, carrots, and onion. Bring to boiling; reduce heat. Cover; simmer about 30 minutes or till vegetables are tender.

Drain meat and vegetables, reserving liquid. Set meat and vegetables aside. Skim off fat from reserved liquid. Add enough water to liquid to equal 1¼ cups; return to the Dutch oven. Combine cold water and cornstarch; stir into liquid in the Dutch oven. Cook and stir till thickened and bubbly. Stir in beef and vegetables. Heat through. Makes 4 (1-cup) servings. One serving equals:

■ ■   **Lean Meat Exchanges**
■   **Starch/Bread Exchange**
■ ■   **Vegetable Exchanges**

MUSTARD-MARINATED STEAK

Mustard and vinegar add zip to the steak.

¾ **pound boneless beef sirloin steak,
    cut 1 inch thick**
2 **tablespoons water**
2 **tablespoons red wine vinegar**
2 **teaspoons cooking oil**
2 **teaspoons Dijon-style mustard**
½ **teaspoon onion salt**
½ **teaspoon dried thyme, crushed**

Trim separable fat from steak. Place meat in a plastic bag set in a bowl.

For marinade, in a small mixing bowl combine the water, vinegar, oil, mustard, onion salt, and thyme. Pour marinade over meat. Close bag. Marinate in the refrigerator for 4 to 24 hours, turning occasionally.

Drain meat, reserving marinade. Place meat on the unheated rack of a broiler pan. Broil 3 inches from the heat for 13 to 17 minutes or to medium doneness, turning once and brushing occasionally with reserved marinade. Transfer meat to a serving platter. Slice thinly across the grain. Makes 4 servings. One serving equals:

▪ ▪ **Lean Meat Exchanges**
▪ **Fat Exchange**

TIJUANA TACO SALAD

Our combination of lean ground beef and spices tastes like sausage, but has less fat.

1 **pound lean ground beef**
¼ **cup chopped onion**
1 **7½-ounce can tomatoes, cut up, *or*
    1 cup peeled and chopped fresh tomato**
2 **teaspoons chili powder**
¼ **teaspoon salt**
¼ **teaspoon garlic powder**
¼ **teaspoon ground cumin**
⅛ **teaspoon pepper**
6 **lettuce leaves**
12 **cups torn lettuce**
1½ **cups chopped tomato**
½ **cup shredded low-fat cheddar cheese *or*
    part-skim mozzarella cheese (2 ounces)**

In a large skillet cook beef and onion till beef is brown. Drain off fat. Stir in *undrained* canned tomatoes or 1 cup chopped fresh tomato, chili powder, salt, garlic powder, cumin, and pepper. Bring to boiling; reduce heat. Simmer, uncovered, till most of the liquid evaporates, stirring occasionally.

Line 6 individual salad bowls with the lettuce leaves. Place torn lettuce in the salad bowls. Spoon beef mixture atop lettuce. Top with chopped tomato. Sprinkle with cheese. Makes 6 servings. One serving equals:

▪ ▪ ▪ **Lean Meat Exchanges**
▪ ▪ **Vegetable Exchanges**

LIME BEEF-AND-CHICKEN KABOBS

Next time use 1 pound of chicken breast halves and omit the beef.

   3 tablespoons frozen apple juice
       concentrate
   3 tablespoons water
   ½ teaspoon finely shredded lime peel
   2 tablespoons lime juice
   ½ teaspoon sesame oil
   ¼ teaspoon salt
   ¼ teaspoon dried thyme, crushed
       Dash ground red pepper (optional)
   ¾ pound boned skinless chicken breast
       halves
   6 ounces boneless beef round steak,
       cut 1 inch thick
   2 cups yellow summer squash or zucchini
       cut into 1-inch pieces
   1 cup sweet red or green pepper
       cut into 1-inch squares
       Nonstick spray coating

For marinade combine apple juice concentrate, the water, lime peel, lime juice, sesame oil, salt, thyme, and, if desired, red pepper. Cut chicken and beef into 1-inch pieces. Place in a plastic bag set in a bowl. Pour marinade over chicken and beef. Close bag and refrigerate for 1 to 4 hours, turning occasionally. Drain, reserving marinade.

On four 15-inch skewers or eight 12-inch skewers thread chicken, beef, squash or zucchini, and pepper. Spray the unheated rack of a broiler pan with nonstick coating. Place kabobs on the rack. Broil 3 to 4 inches from the heat for 5 minutes. Brush with reserved marinade. Turn kabobs over. Broil 4 to 6 minutes more or till chicken is tender and no longer pink.

Bring remaining marinade to boiling. Reduce heat and simmer for 1 minute. Strain; drizzle marinade over kabobs. Makes 4 servings. One serving equals:

       Lean Meat Exchanges
   ▮ **Fruit Exchange**
   ▮ **Vegetable Exchange**

STEAK WITH MARSALA SAUCE

Broiling, a lean-cooking technique, keeps this tasty recipe in your diet.

   1 pound boneless beef sirloin steak,
       cut 1 inch thick
       Nonstick spray coating
   1 cup sliced fresh mushrooms
   ½ cup sliced onion, separated into rings
   ⅓ cup dry Marsala
   ¼ cup water
   2 tablespoons snipped parsley
   ½ teaspoon instant beef bouillon granules
       Dash ground pepper
       Tomato roses (optional)
       Parsley sprigs (optional)

Trim separable fat from steak. Place steak on the unheated rack of a broiler pan. Broil 3 inches from the heat for 5 minutes. Turn and broil 3 to 7 minutes more for rare or 8 to 12 minutes more for medium.

Meanwhile, for sauce spray a *cold* medium saucepan with nonstick coating. Preheat the saucepan over medium heat. Add mushrooms and onion. Cook and stir till tender. Stir in Marsala, the water, snipped parsley, beef bouillon granules, and pepper. Bring to boiling. Boil gently, uncovered, about 4 minutes or till liquid is reduced to ¾ cup.

To serve, slice steak. Serve sauce over steak slices. If desired, garnish with tomato roses and parsley sprigs. Makes 4 servings. One serving equals:

       Lean Meat Exchanges
   ▮ **Vegetable Exchange**

Steak with Marsala Sauce

BEEF BURGUNDY

Use a fresh mushroom or two as attractive garnishes for your serving platter.

1 pound boneless beef sirloin steak
Nonstick spray coating
¾ cup sliced onion
½ cup water
½ cup burgundy
1 bay leaf
1½ teaspoons instant beef bouillon granules
¼ teaspoon dried thyme, crushed
⅛ teaspoon pepper
2 cups sliced fresh mushrooms
2 tablespoons cold water
4 teaspoons cornstarch
2 cups hot cooked noodles
2 tablespoons snipped parsley

Trim separable fat from steak. Partially freeze beef. Thinly slice, across the grain, into bite-size strips.

Spray a *cold* large saucepan with nonstick coating. Preheat over medium heat. Cook *half* of the beef over medium heat till brown. Remove beef. Repeat with remaining beef. Return all the beef to the saucepan.

Stir in onion, the ½ cup water, burgundy, bay leaf, bouillon granules, thyme, and pepper. Bring to boiling; reduce heat. Cover and simmer for 20 minutes. Add mushrooms; cook for 5 to 10 minutes more or till beef is tender. Remove bay leaf.

Stir together the 2 tablespoons cold water and cornstarch. Add to beef mixture. Cook and stir till thickened and bubbly. Cook and stir for 2 minutes more. Serve beef mixture over hot cooked noodles. Sprinkle with snipped parsley. Makes 4 (1¼-cup) servings. One serving equals:

■ ■ ■ **Lean Meat Exchanges**
▮ ■ **Starch/Bread Exchanges**
■ **Vegetable Exchange**

SAVORY STEAK AND GRAVY

If you like, serve this over hot rice or toast points. One serving of either equals 1 Bread Exchange.

1 pound boneless beef round steak, cut ¾ inch thick
2 tablespoons all-purpose flour
1½ teaspoons dry mustard
¼ teaspoon pepper
Nonstick spray coating
1 cup sliced fresh mushrooms
½ cup water
1 teaspoon Worcestershire sauce
½ teaspoon instant beef bouillon granules

Trim separable fat from the steak. With a sharp knife cut the steak into 4 serving-size pieces. In a small mixing bowl stir together the flour, dry mustard, and pepper. With a meat mallet pound the flour mixture into the steak pieces.

Spray a *cold* large skillet with nonstick coating. Preheat the skillet over medium heat. Add the steak pieces to the skillet. Brown on both sides.

Stir in sliced mushrooms, water, Worcestershire sauce, and instant beef bouillon granules. Bring to boiling; reduce heat. Cover the skillet and simmer about 1¼ hours or till the meat is tender. Makes 4 servings. One serving equals:

■ ■ ■ **Lean Meat Exchanges**

ROUND STEAK STROGANOFF

Using low-fat yogurt instead of sour cream reduces the fat in this traditional dish.

¾ pound boneless beef top round steak, cut ¾ inch thick
1 8-ounce carton plain low-fat yogurt
2 tablespoons cornstarch
⅓ cup water
1 tablespoon tomato paste
2 teaspoons instant beef bouillon granules
  Nonstick spray coating
1 cup sliced fresh mushrooms
½ cup shredded carrot
½ cup sliced green onion
1 clove garlic, minced
2 tablespoons dry red wine
2 cups hot cooked noodles

Trim separable fat from steak. Partially freeze the beef. Thinly slice, across the grain, into bite-size strips. In a small bowl combine yogurt and cornstarch. Stir in water, tomato paste, and bouillon granules; set aside.

Spray a *cold* large skillet with nonstick coating. Preheat the skillet over medium heat. Quickly brown the meat. Remove meat from the skillet.

Add mushrooms, carrot, green onion, and garlic to the skillet. Cook and stir till the onion is tender.

Add meat to the vegetable mixture. Add the yogurt mixture. Cook and stir till mixture is thickened and bubbly. Cook and stir 2 minutes more. Stir in the dry red wine. Serve over hot noodles. Makes 4 (1½-cup) servings. One serving equals:

▪ ▪ ▪   **Lean Meat Exchanges**
▪ ▪   **Starch/Bread Exchanges**
▪   **Vegetable Exchange**
▪   **Milk Exchange**
▪   **Fat Exchange**

TACO COMPUESTO

Make these tacos in less than 20 minutes.

¾ pound lean ground beef
½ cup chopped onion
2 tablespoons canned diced green chili peppers
1 clove garlic, minced
1 teaspoon chili powder
1½ cups chopped tomato
3 tablespoons reduced-calorie Italian salad dressing
½ teaspoon seasoned salt
8 taco shells
1 cup shredded lettuce
½ cup shredded low-calorie process cheese *or* part-skim mozzarella cheese (2 ounces)
½ cup taco sauce

In a large skillet cook ground beef, chopped onion, green chili peppers, and minced garlic over medium heat till beef is brown. Drain off fat. Stir in chili powder.

In a mixing bowl combine chopped tomato, Italian salad dressing, and seasoned salt.

Spoon beef mixture into taco shells. Top with tomato mixture, shredded lettuce, shredded cheese, and taco sauce. Makes 4 servings. One serving equals:

▪ ▪ ▪   **Lean Meat Exchanges**
▪   **Starch/Bread Exchange**
▪   **Vegetable Exchange**
▪ ▪   **Fat Exchanges**

STIR-FRIED BEEF AND SPINACH

Use purchased five-spice powder or make your own, using the recipe in the box below.

¾ pound boneless beef round steak
2 teaspoons cornstarch
2 tablespoons reduced-sodium soy sauce
¼ teaspoon five-spice powder
¼ teaspoon instant beef bouillon granules
Nonstick spray coating
¼ cup sliced green onion
1 teaspoon grated gingerroot
1 tablespoon cooking oil
6 cups torn spinach
½ cup sliced water chestnuts

Trim separable fat from steak. Partially freeze. Thinly slice, across grain, into bite-size strips. Set aside. Combine cornstarch and ¼ cup *water*. Stir in soy sauce, five-spice powder, and bouillon granules. Set aside. Spray a *cold* wok with nonstick coating. Preheat over medium heat. Stir-fry onion and gingerroot for 30 seconds. Add oil. Add beef; stir-fry 3 minutes. Stir cornstarch mixture; stir into beef. Cook and stir till thickened and bubbly. Stir in spinach and water chestnuts. Cook, covered, 1 to 2 minutes or till spinach wilts. Makes 4 (⅔-cup) servings. One serving equals:

Lean Meat Exchanges
Vegetable Exchange
Fat Exchange

FIVE-SPICE POWDER

For homemade five-spice powder, combine 1 teaspoon ground *cinnamon*; 1 teaspoon crushed *aniseed* or 1 *anise*, ground; ¼ teaspoon crushed *fennel seed*; ¼ teaspoon *pepper* or crushed *Szechwan pepper*; and ⅛ teaspoon ground *cloves*. Store in a covered container.

SPAGHETTI SQUASH WITH TOMATO SAUCE

Swap lower-calorie spaghetti squash for pasta.

1 2½-pound spaghetti squash
1 pound lean ground beef *or* turkey
½ cup chopped onion
1 clove garlic, minced
1 28-ounce can tomatoes, cut up
¼ cup dry red wine
1 bay leaf
2 tablespoons snipped parsley
1 teaspoon dried basil, crushed
1 teaspoon instant beef bouillon granules
½ teaspoon dried oregano, crushed
¼ teaspoon dried thyme, crushed
⅛ teaspoon pepper
2 cups sliced fresh mushrooms
1 tablespoon water
2 teaspoons cornstarch
¼ cup chopped tomato (optional)
Fresh basil leaves (optional)

Cut the squash in half lengthwise; remove seeds and strings. In a baking dish place squash halves, cut side down. With a fork prick the skin all over. Bake in a 350° oven for 30 to 40 minutes or till tender.

Meanwhile, for sauce, in a saucepan cook beef or turkey, onion, and garlic till meat is brown. Drain off fat. Stir in *undrained* tomatoes, wine, bay leaf, parsley, dried basil, bouillon granules, oregano, thyme, and pepper. Bring to boiling; reduce heat. Simmer, uncovered, for 40 minutes, stirring occasionally. Stir in mushrooms. Cook for 10 minutes. Remove bay leaf.

Combine water and cornstarch. Stir into beef mixture. Cook and stir till bubbly. Cook and stir for 2 minutes more.

Using two forks, shred and separate the squash pulp into strands. Serve sauce atop strands. If desired, garnish with chopped tomato and fresh basil. Makes 6 (1¼-cup) servings. One serving equals:

Lean Meat Exchanges
Vegetable Exchanges

Spaghetti Squash with Tomato Sauce

ONE-POT SPAGHETTI

Use just one pan to make a complete spaghetti dinner.

1 pound lean ground beef
3 cups water
2¼ cups tomato juice
1 6-ounce can tomato paste
2 tablespoons dried minced onion
1 teaspoon salt
1 teaspoon garlic powder
1 teaspoon dried basil, crushed
1 teaspoon dried oregano, crushed
  Several dashes bottled hot pepper sauce
1 7-ounce package spaghetti, broken
7 tablespoons grated Parmesan cheese

In a Dutch oven cook the ground beef till brown. Drain off fat. Stir in the water, tomato juice, tomato paste, dried minced onion, salt, garlic powder, dried basil, dried oregano, and bottled hot pepper sauce. Bring mixture to boiling.

Add spaghetti to the boiling mixture, a little at a time. Reduce heat. Simmer, covered, for 30 minutes, stirring often. Serve with grated Parmesan cheese. Makes 7 (1-cup) servings. One serving equals:

  Lean Meat Exchanges
  Starch/Bread Exchange
  Vegetable Exchanges
  Fat Exchange

BEEF SLAW-WICHES

Speed up preparation by buying already-shredded cabbage instead of shredding your own.

⅓ cup reduced-calorie Thousand Island salad dressing
1 teaspoon prepared mustard
½ teaspoon caraway seed
2 cups finely shredded cabbage
2 tablespoons sliced green onion
8 slices very thin white or whole wheat bread
8 ounces thinly sliced cooked roast beef

Stir together Thousand Island salad dressing, prepared mustard, and caraway seed. Combine shredded cabbage and green onion; toss with the salad dressing mixture.

Toast bread slices. For sandwiches, spoon about ¼ cup of the cabbage mixture onto 4 of the toasted bread slices. Arrange the beef slices atop sandwiches. Spoon about ¼ cup of the cabbage mixture atop each beef slice. Top with the remaining toasted bread slices. Makes 4 servings. One serving equals:

  Lean Meat Exchanges
  Starch/Bread Exchange
  Vegetable Exchange
  Fat Exchanges

VEAL CHOPS WITH VEGETABLES

4 veal top loin chops, cut ½ inch thick (1¼ pounds total)
  Nonstick spray coating
1 16-ounce package loose-pack frozen broccoli, red pepper, bamboo shoots, and straw mushrooms
½ cup water
1 clove garlic, minced
1 teaspoon instant chicken bouillon granules
¼ teaspoon ground ginger
2 tablespoons water
2 teaspoons cornstarch

Trim separable fat from veal chops. Spray a *cold* large skillet with nonstick coating. Preheat the skillet over medium heat. Cook veal chops in skillet over medium heat for 4 to 6 minutes or till veal is no longer pink, turning once. Transfer cooked chops to a platter; cover to keep warm.

Stir the frozen vegetables, ½ cup water, garlic, chicken bouillon granules, and ginger into skillet. Bring mixture to boiling, stirring to scrape up browned bits from bottom. Reduce heat. Cover and simmer for 2 minutes.

In a small mixing bowl stir together the 2 tablespoons water and cornstarch. Stir into the mixture in the skillet. Cook and stir till thickened and bubbly. Cook and stir for 2 minutes more. Serve with veal. Makes 4 servings. One serving equals:

    Lean Meat Exchanges
  Vegetable Exchange

VEAL SCALLOPINI

Veal and mushrooms–perfect for company!

¾ pound boneless veal leg round steak, cut ¼ inch thick
  Nonstick spray coating
3 tablespoons dry sherry
2 tablespoons water
¾ teaspoon instant chicken bouillon granules
  Dash pepper
2 cups sliced fresh mushrooms
1 tablespoon snipped parsley

Trim separable fat from veal steak. Cut veal into 4 pieces; pound to ⅛-inch thickness.

Spray a *cold* 12-inch skillet with nonstick coating. Preheat skillet over medium heat. Cook veal in hot skillet for 2 to 3 minutes or till no longer pink, turning once. Remove from skillet; cover with foil to keep warm.

For sauce, in the same skillet stir together dry sherry, water, instant chicken bouillon granules, and pepper. Stir in mushrooms. Bring to boiling, stirring to scrape up browned bits from bottom. Boil, uncovered, about 3 minutes or till most of the liquid has evaporated. Pour over veal. Sprinkle with snipped parsley. Makes 4 servings. One serving equals:

    Lean Meat Exchanges
  Vegetable Exchange

VEAL AND PEPPERS ITALIANO

Next time substitute boneless pork loin for the veal.

    1 pound boneless lean veal
       Nonstick spray coating
    1 14½-ounce can tomatoes, cut up
    ½ cup water
    2 tablespoons sliced leek *or* green onion
    2 cloves garlic, minced
    1 teaspoon dried basil, crushed
    ½ teaspoon instant chicken bouillon
         granules
    ½ teaspoon dried oregano, crushed
    ⅛ teaspoon salt
    ⅛ teaspoon pepper
   1½ cups green pepper cut into bite-size strips
    2 tablespoons water
    1 tablespoon cornstarch
    2 cups hot cooked noodles

Trim separable fat from veal. Cut into 1-inch cubes. Spray a *cold* large skillet with nonstick coating. Preheat skillet over medium heat. Brown veal in the hot skillet.

Stir in *undrained* tomatoes, water, sliced leek or green onion, garlic, basil, chicken bouillon granules, oregano, salt, and pepper. Bring to boiling; reduce heat. Simmer, covered, for 15 minutes. Add green peppers. Cook, covered, for 5 to 10 minutes or till peppers are tender.

Stir together 2 tablespoons water and cornstarch. Stir into meat mixture. Cook and stir till mixture is thickened and bubbly. Cook and stir 2 minutes more. Serve with hot cooked noodles. Makes 4 (1½-cup) servings. One serving equals:

    ▪ ▪ ▪   **Lean Meat Exchanges**
    ▪ ▪   **Starch/Bread Exchanges**
    ▪ ▪   **Vegetable Exchanges**

LEAN VEAL PARMESAN

Limiting the cheese and fat, but not the flavor, makes this a dieter's treat.

    ¾ pound boneless veal leg round steak, cut
         ¼ inch thick, *or* turkey breast slices
    2 tablespoons all-purpose flour
    2 tablespoons yellow cornmeal
    1 tablespoon grated Parmesan cheese
    ½ teaspoon garlic salt
    ½ teaspoon dried oregano, crushed
    ⅛ teaspoon pepper
       Nonstick spray coating
    4 tomato slices
    1 tablespoon grated Parmesan cheese

Trim separable fat from veal. Cut veal into 4 serving-size pieces. Rinse veal or turkey slices under running water; shake off excess water. Combine flour, yellow cornmeal, 1 tablespoon Parmesean cheese, garlic salt, oregano, and pepper. Coat veal or turkey with the cornmeal mixture.

Spray a shallow baking pan with nonstick coating. Arrange veal or turkey in baking pan. Bake in a 400° oven for 20 minutes for veal or 15 minutes for turkey. Top each piece of veal or turkey with a tomato slice. Sprinkle with 1 tablespoon Parmesan cheese. Bake for 2 to 3 minutes more or till veal or turkey are tender and no longer pink. Makes 4 servings. One serving equals:

    ▪ ▪ ▪   **Lean Meat Exchanges**
    ▪   **Starch/Bread Exchange**

PINEAPPLE AND PORK STIR-FRY

Pick juice-pack pineapple—it contains less sugar than syrup-packed.

¾ pound pork tenderloin *or* boneless pork
1 20-ounce can whole pineapple (juice pack)
2 tablespoons reduced-sodium soy sauce
1 clove garlic, minced
½ teaspoon instant chicken bouillon granules
⅛ teaspoon pepper
1 tablespoon cornstarch
   Nonstick spray coating
1 cup sweet red *or* green pepper cut into 1-inch squares

Trim separable fat from the pork. Partially freeze pork. Thinly slice, across the grain, into bite-size strips. Set aside. Drain pineapple, reserving juice. Cut pineapple lengthwise into 8 wedges. In a small bowl combine ½ *cup* of the reserved pineapple juice, the soy sauce, garlic, bouillon granules, and pepper; set aside. In small bowl stir remaining pineapple juice into the cornstarch; set aside.

Spray a *cold* wok or large skillet with nonstick coating. Preheat over medium heat. Add pork; stir-fry for 3 to 4 minutes or till pork is just brown. Remove from wok. Add pepper squares to wok; stir-fry about 2 minutes or till crisp-tender. Remove from wok.

Pour soy sauce mixture into wok; add pineapple wedges. Cook, covered, for 2 minutes. Remove wedges with a slotted spoon and arrange on a platter; keep warm.

Return pork and peppers to hot liquid in the wok. Stir cornstarch mixture; add to wok. Cook and stir till thickened and bubbly. Cook and stir 2 minutes more. Spoon pork mixture atop pineapple wedges. Makes 4 (½-cup) servings. One serving equals:

    Lean Meat Exchanges
∎ ∎ **Fruit Exchanges**

To make slicing the pork easier, freeze the meat for about 20 minutes. Then, cut into thin slices.

BARBECUED HAM SLICE

½ cup orange juice
1 tablespoon dry sherry
1 teaspoon cornstarch
¾ pound fully cooked ham slice, cut ¾ inch thick
¾ cup seedless red *or* green grapes, halved

For sauce, in a small saucepan stir together orange juice, sherry, and cornstarch. Cook and stir till the mixture is thickened and bubbly. Cook and stir for 2 minutes more.

Trim separable fat from ham. Place ham on the unheated rack of a broiler pan. Brush with *1 tablespoon* of the sauce. Broil 3 to 4 inches from the heat for 5 minutes; turn. Brush with *1 tablespoon* of the sauce. Broil 4 to 5 minutes more or till the ham is heated through. Meanwhile, stir the grape halves into the remaining sauce. Heat through. Spoon sauce over ham to serve. Makes 4 servings. One serving equals:

    Lean Meat Exchanges
∎ **Fruit Exchange**

SPICY MARINATED PORK CHOPS

Serve these peppy chops with steamed zucchini or a tossed green salad.

4 pork loin chops, cut ½ inch thick
    (1¼ pounds total)
1 6-ounce can (¾ cup) vegetable juice
    cocktail
3 tablespoons finely chopped onion
3 tablespoons canned diced green chili
    peppers
2 teaspoons Worcestershire sauce
½ teaspoon dried Italian seasoning, crushed
⅛ teaspoon garlic powder
    Few drops bottled hot pepper sauce
1⅓ cups hot cooked rice

Trim separable fat from pork chops. For marinade, combine vegetable juice cocktail, onion, green chili peppers, Worcestershire sauce, Italian seasoning, garlic powder, and bottled hot pepper sauce.

Place a plastic bag in a medium mixing bowl. Put the chops in the plastic bag. Pour marinade over chops. Close bag. Marinate in the refrigerator for 2 to 24 hours, turning occasionally to coat all sides of the chops.

Drain chops; reserve marinade. Place chops on the unheated rack of a broiler pan. Broil 3 to 4 inches from the heat for 4 minutes. Turn chops; broil for 4 to 8 minutes more or till no pink remains.

Meanwhile, in a small saucepan bring reserved marinade to boiling. Serve the hot marinade with the pork chops and rice. Makes 4 servings. One serving equals:

    Lean Meat Exchanges
    Starch/Bread Exchange
    Vegetable Exchange

SKILLET POTATO DINNER

Super-easy, super-fast, and super-good!

1 10-ounce package frozen cut broccoli
1½ cups skim milk
1 tablespoon cornstarch
½ teaspoon dry mustard
½ teaspoon dried basil, crushed
¼ teaspoon pepper
2 cups frozen loose-pack hash brown
    potatoes, thawed
½ pound cubed fully cooked ham (1½ cups)
¼ cup grated Parmesan cheese

In a large skillet cook the frozen broccoli according to the package directions. Drain broccoli and set aside.

In a small mixing bowl stir together *2 tablespoons* of the skim milk, the cornstarch, dry mustard, dried basil, and pepper. In the skillet stir together the cornstarch mixture and the remaining milk. Cook and stir over medium heat till the mixture is thickened and bubbly. Cook and stir for 2 minutes more.

Stir in cooked broccoli, thawed hash brown potatoes, ham cubes, and *2 tablespoons* of the grated Parmesan cheese. Cover and cook till the mixture is heated through, stirring occasionally. Sprinkle with the remaining Parmesan cheese before serving. Makes 4 (1¼-cup) servings. One serving equals:

    Lean Meat Exchanges
    Starch/Bread Exchange
    Vegetable Exchange
    Milk Exchange

PASTA-HAM SALAD
Tastes like a delicious deli salad.

4   ounces corkscrew macaroni
¼   cup vinegar
¼   cup unsweetened orange *or* apple juice
1   tablespoon salad oil
½   teaspoon dry mustard
½   teaspoon dried basil, crushed
⅛   teaspoon pepper
1   cup sliced fresh mushrooms
1   cup chopped, seeded tomato
¼   pound cubed fully cooked ham (¾ cup)
½   cup shredded low-fat cheddar cheese
      (2 ounces)
4   lettuce leaves

Cook the corkscrew macaroni according to the package directions. Drain. Rinse with cold water; drain.

Meanwhile, for dressing, in a screw-top jar combine vinegar, orange or apple juice, salad oil, dry mustard, basil, and pepper. Cover and shake well to mix.

Transfer the macaroni to a medium mixing bowl. Pour the dressing over the macaroni; toss gently to coat. Cover and chill in the refrigerator for 2 to 24 hours.

To serve, add sliced mushrooms, chopped tomato, ham cubes, and cheddar cheese to the macaroni mixture. Toss gently to mix. Serve on lettuce-lined plates. Makes 4 (1¼-cup) servings. One serving equals:

■ **Lean Meat Exchanges**
■ **Starch/Bread Exchange**
■ **Vegetable Exchange**
■ **Fat Exchange**

CAJUN PORK PINWHEELS
Like spicy foods? Then, give these a try.

¾   pound pork tenderloin
      Nonstick spray coating
½   cup finely chopped sweet red, yellow,
      or green pepper
¼   cup finely chopped onion
¼   cup finely chopped celery
½   teaspoon dried thyme, crushed
½   teaspoon fennel seed
¼   teaspoon garlic salt
¼   teaspoon paprika
⅛   to ¼ teaspoon pepper
      Dash ground red pepper

Trim separable fat and the paper-thin membrane from the surface of the tenderloin. Use a sharp knife to cut tenderloin lengthwise to, but not through, the other side. Cover with plastic wrap. Use the flat side of a meat mallet to pound the tenderloin, working from the center to edges, to make a 12x8-inch rectangle. Remove plastic wrap. Set the tenderloin aside.

Spray a *cold* medium skillet with nonstick coating. Preheat the skillet over medium heat. Add chopped pepper, onion, celery, thyme, fennel seed, garlic salt, paprika, pepper, and ground red pepper. Cook, stirring frequently, about 4 minutes or till vegetables are tender. Remove from the heat.

Spread the vegetable mixture evenly over tenderloin to within ½ inch of the edge. Roll up from one of the short sides. Secure the meat roll with wooden toothpicks or tie with string at 1-inch intervals. Cut the meat roll into nine slices.

Place meat slices on the unheated rack of a broiler pan, cut sides down. Broil 4 inches from the heat for 5 minutes. Turn; broil for 5 to 8 minutes more or till no pink remains in meat. Remove toothpicks or string. Makes 3 servings. One serving equals:

■ ■ ■ ■ **Lean Meat Exchanges**
■ **Vegetable Exchange**

61

Pork Medaillons
with Apple-
Yogurt Sauce

PORK MEDAILLONS WITH APPLE-YOGURT SAUCE

Pork + Apples = Good Eating.

¾ **pound pork tenderloin**
 Nonstick spray coating
1 **cup thinly sliced apple**
½ **cup unsweetened apple juice**
⅓ **cup chopped onion**
¼ **teaspoon salt**
¼ **teaspoon dried sage, crushed**
1 **8-ounce carton plain low-fat yogurt**
2 **tablespoons all-purpose flour**
2 **cups hot cooked fettuccine *or* noodles**
 Snipped chives (optional)
 Sage sprigs (optional)
1 **tiny red onion, cut in half (optional)**

Trim separable fat from pork. Cut pork into 1-inch slices. Place each piece of pork between 2 sheets of plastic wrap. Lightly pound with the flat side of a meat mallet to ½-inch thickness.

Spray a *cold* large skillet with nonstick coating. Preheat the skillet over medium heat. Add pork slices to the skillet; cook over medium heat for 3 minutes. Turn pork. Cook for 3 to 4 minutes more or till no pink remains. Remove pork from skillet; keep warm.

For sauce, add apple slices, apple juice, chopped onion, salt, and dried sage to skillet. Cook, covered, about 5 minutes or till onion is tender. Stir together yogurt and flour. Add yogurt mixture to skillet. Cook and stir till thickened and bubbly. Cook and stir for 1 minute more. Arrange pork atop fettuccine or noodles. Spoon sauce over pork and pasta. If desired, sprinkle with chives and garnish with fresh sage and red onion halves. Makes 4 servings. One serving equals:

  Lean Meat Exchanges
■ ■ **Starch/Bread Exchanges**
■ **Fruit Exchange**
  Milk Exchange

CHEF'S SALAD BOWL

Select a salad dressing with no more than 25 calories per tablespoon.

¼ **pound fully cooked ham**
1½ **cups thinly sliced cauliflower flowerets**
½ **cup sliced radishes**
½ **cup sliced green onions**
½ **cup reduced-calorie Italian, French, creamy cucumber, *or* other salad dressing**
4 **cups torn mixed greens**
4 **ounces low-fat cheddar cheese, cut into julienne strips**
⅔ **cup halved cherry tomatoes**

Trim separable fat from ham. Use a sharp knife to cut the ham into julienne strips.

In a large mixing bowl combine cauliflower flowerets, radishes, and green onions. Add salad dressing; toss to coat. Set aside.

To serve, place torn greens in 4 individual salad bowls. Arrange the cauliflower mixture, ham strips, cheddar cheese strips, and cherry tomato halves atop the greens. Makes 4 (1¼-cup) servings. One serving equals:

  Lean Meat Exchange
  Vegetable Exchange
■ **Fat Exchange**

HAM BURRITOS

½ cup low-fat cottage cheese
2 tablespoons chopped green pepper
1 tablespoon sliced green onion
2 6-inch flour tortillas
1 teaspoon Dijon-style mustard
2 ounces thinly sliced fully cooked ham

Stir together cottage cheese, green pepper, and green onion; set aside.

Spread *each* tortilla with *½ teaspoon* of the mustard. Arrange ham on *each* tortilla. Spoon *half* of the cottage cheese mixture onto *each* tortilla near one edge. Fold bottom of tortilla over cottage cheese mixture; roll up jelly-roll style. If necessary, secure with wooden toothpicks. Serve immediately or wrap and chill up to 2 hours. Makes 2 servings. One serving equals:

    ■ ■ **Lean Meat Exchanges**
    ■ **Starch/Bread Exchange**
    ▮ **Fat Exchange**

FRUITED HAM TOSS

1 cup sliced apple
3 cups torn mixed greens
1 6-ounce package sliced fully cooked ham, cut into strips
½ cup seedless red *or* green grapes, halved
¼ cup chopped celery
¼ cup reduced-calorie buttermilk salad dressing

Cut apple slices in half. Combine apple, greens, ham, grapes, and celery. Toss to mix. Add salad dressing; toss to coat. Makes 3 (2-cup) servings. One serving equals:

    ■ ■ **Lean Meat Exchanges**
    ▮ **Fruit Exchange**
    ■ **Vegetable Exchange**
    ■ **Fat Exchange**

LAMB CHOPS WITH PEACHES

Smother your lamb chops in a tangy peach sauce.

2 teaspoons cornstarch
¼ teaspoon ground nutmeg
Dash ground ginger
½ cup unsweetened orange juice
2 tablespoons water
1 teaspoon reduced-sodium soy sauce
8 lamb loin chops, cut ¾ inch thick
1 cup peeled, pitted, and coarsely chopped peaches *or* 1 cup chopped frozen unsweetened peach slices

For sauce, in a small saucepan combine cornstarch, nutmeg, and ginger. Stir in orange juice, water, and soy sauce. Cook and stir over medium heat till mixture is thickened and bubbly. Cook and stir for 2 minutes more. Remove from heat.

Trim separable fat from lamb chops. Place chops on the unheated rack of a broiler pan. Brush chops with some of the sauce. Broil 3 to 4 inches from the heat for 4 minutes. Turn chops; brush with sauce. Broil for 5 to 6 minutes more or till no pink remains in meat.

Meanwhile, stir peaches into the remaining sauce; heat through. Serve sauce with chops. Makes 8 servings. One serving equals:

    ■ ■ **Lean Meat Exchanges**
    ▮ **Fruit Exchange**

ATHENIAN LAMB KABOBS

Only four ingredients make this tangy marinade.

¾ cup reduced-calorie French salad dressing
3 tablespoons lime juice
½ teaspoon dried oregano, crushed
¼ teaspoon dried tarragon, crushed
1½ pounds lean boneless lamb
2 cups small fresh mushrooms
2 cups green pepper cut into 1-inch pieces
Snipped parsley (optional)

For marinade, in a small mixing bowl stir together French salad dressing, lime juice, oregano, and tarragon; set aside.

Trim separable fat from the lamb. Cut lamb into 1-inch cubes. Place a plastic bag in a medium mixing bowl. Put the lamb cubes in the plastic bag. Pour marinade over meat in bag. Close bag. Marinate in the refrigerator for 2 hours, turning the bag occasionally to coat all cubes.

Drain lamb cubes; reserve marinade. Pour boiling water over mushrooms. Let stand 1 minute; drain.

On six 10- to 12-inch skewers alternately thread lamb, mushrooms, and green pepper. Place on the unheated rack of a broiler pan. Broil 4 to 5 inches from the heat about 15 minutes or till no pink remains in meat, turning and brushing occasionally with reserved marinade. (Or, grill kabobs on an uncovered grill over hot coals for 8 to 12 minutes or till no pink remains in meat, turning and brushing occasionally with reserved marinade.) If desired, sprinkle kabobs with snipped parsley. Makes 6 servings. One serving equals:

■ ■ ■   **Lean Meat Exchanges**
■   **Vegetable Exchange**
■ ■   **Fat Exchanges**

TOFU AND BROCCOLI STIR-FRY

Look for tofu in the produce section of your supermarket.

⅔ cup water
2 tablespoons dry sherry
2 tablespoons reduced-sodium soy sauce
4 teaspoons cornstarch
¼ teaspoon ground ginger
¼ teaspoon crushed red pepper
Nonstick spray coating
2 cloves garlic, minced
3 cups broccoli cut into bite-size pieces
½ cup onion cut into wedges
1 cup fresh bean sprouts
1 pound fresh tofu (bean curd), cut into ½-inch cubes
1⅓ cups hot cooked brown rice

For sauce, stir together water, sherry, soy sauce, cornstarch, ginger, and red pepper; set aside.

Spray a *cold* wok or large skillet with nonstick coating. Preheat the wok or skillet over medium heat. Add garlic; stir-fry for 15 seconds. Add broccoli; stir-fry for 3 minutes. Add onion; stir-fry for 3 minutes. Add bean sprouts; stir-fry for 1 minute. Push vegetables from the center of the wok or skillet.

Stir sauce; add to the center of the wok or skillet. Cook and stir till thickened and bubbly. Cook and stir for 2 minutes more. Stir vegetables into sauce; stir in tofu. Heat through. Serve with rice. Makes 4 (1½-cup) servings. One serving equals:

■   **Lean Meat Exchange**
■   **Starch/Bread Exchange**
■ ■   **Vegetable Exchanges**
■   **Fat Exchange**

SALSA-TOPPED FRITTATA

Our frittata contains just one egg yolk, making it lower in calories and cholesterol than most egg dishes.

5 egg whites
1 egg
1 tablespoon snipped cilantro *or* parsley
¼ teaspoon salt
⅛ teaspoon pepper
Nonstick spray coating
1 cup sliced fresh mushrooms
½ cup sliced onion
⅓ cup red salsa
½ cup shredded low-fat cheddar cheese
    (2 ounces)

In a medium mixing bowl lightly beat together egg whites and whole egg. Stir in snipped cilantro or parsley, salt, and pepper; set aside.

Spray a *cold* 8-inch ovenproof skillet with nonstick coating. Preheat the skillet over medium heat. Add mushrooms and onion to the hot skillet. Cook for 3 to 4 minutes or till mushrooms and onion are tender. Remove skillet from heat.

Pour egg mixture evenly over vegetables in the skillet. Bake, uncovered, in a 350° oven for 6 to 8 minutes or till eggs are set. Spoon salsa over eggs. Sprinkle with cheese. Bake 1 to 2 minutes more or till cheese melts. Makes 3 servings. One serving equals:

■ ■ **Lean Meat Exchanges**
■ **Vegetable Exchange**
■ **Fat Exchange**

EGGS FLORENTINE

Nonstick spray coating
1 cup sliced fresh mushrooms
⅓ cup sliced green onions
¼ cup shredded carrot
1 cup skim milk
4 teaspoons cornstarch
1 teaspoon instant chicken bouillon
    granules
⅛ teaspoon dried tarragon, crushed
2 tablespoons dry white wine
½ of a 9-ounce package frozen chopped
    spinach, thawed and well drained
2 English muffins, split and toasted
4 eggs

For sauce, spray a *cold* medium saucepan with nonstick coating. Preheat saucepan over medium heat. Add mushrooms, green onions, and shredded carrot; cook and stir till tender. Stir together milk, cornstarch, bouillon granules, and tarragon. Stir into vegetable mixture in saucepan. Cook and stir till thickened and bubbly. Cook and stir for 2 minutes more. Stir in wine.

Remove ¾ *cup* of the sauce; keep warm. Add spinach to the remaining sauce in the pan. Cook and stir till bubbly. Spoon *one-fourth* of the spinach mixture onto *each* English muffin half. Keep warm in a 300° oven.

Meanwhile, in another medium saucepan add water to half-fill the pan. Bring to boiling; reduce heat to simmering. Break *one* egg into a measuring cup. Carefully slide egg into simmering water. Repeat with remaining eggs. Simmer, uncovered, for 3 to 5 minutes or to desired doneness. Remove eggs with slotted spoon. Place an egg on *each* muffin half. Top *each* egg with *3 tablespoons* of the reserved sauce. If desired, garnish each serving with a carrot curl and parsley sprig. Makes 4 servings. One serving equals:

□ **Lean Meat Exchange**
■ **Starch/Bread Exchange**
▌ **Vegetable Exchange**
▌ **Fat Exchange**

Eggs
Florentine

EATING AWAY FROM HOME

Because of work schedules and family activities, some of your meals may be eaten away from home. Whether you pack a sack lunch or dine in a restaurant, these meals are as important to your diet as the meals you eat at home.

Calling All Brown Baggers

When you prepare a meal to tote, you control the foods that go into it. That's a big plus for dieters. With a little know-how, your meal will be delicious, safe to eat, and the right temperature at serving time.

Explore Your Options. Your brown bag options are many. Choose a main-dish salad, such as *Turkey Waldorf Salad* (see recipe, page 35), or for a special treat, try *Fruited Crab Salad* (see recipe, page 43). Fix the salads ahead of time, except do not add the salad greens and dressing. Pack them in separate containers and add to the salad ingredients just before you eat.

In the winter months, carry tummy-warming lunches, such as *Old-Fashioned Beef Stew* (see recipe, page 48), in insulated vacuum bottles.

Or, you may prefer a sandwich. Pack lettuce, tomato slices, and saucy fillings separate from the bread and assemble your sandwich at lunchtime. For 1,000- or 1,200-calorie diets, you may want to borrow a Starch/Bread Exchange from breakfast so you can have 2 slices of bread for a sandwich at lunch.

Add fresh fruit for dessert. And for a beverage, try carbonated water, fruit juice, or a diet soft drink packed in convenient single-serving cans, bottles, or cartons.

Safety First. Take time to follow these simple precautions and you will keep your meal safe from harmful bacteria.

- Use very clean utensils and dishes in preparing the food.
- Seal foods in clean airtight containers or plastic storage bags.
- Keep your cold foods cold and your hot foods hot. (Refer to the directions below.)
- Keep your meal in a cool, dry place and eat it within 5 hours.

Keeping Foods the Right Temperature. Cold foods are popular for toting because they are easy to eat at your desk, in the car, or any other place. If you have a refrigerator where you work, chill your meal until you're ready to eat. Otherwise, chill the food thoroughly before packing and put it in an insulated lunch box with a frozen ice pack. You may want to purchase several of the blue plastic ice packs designed for coolers. Just freeze them beforehand and pack the frozen ice packs with the food in your insulated lunch box. Your lunch will stay cold up to 5 hours.

For hot foods, such as soups and stews, just before you leave home, heat the food till all the solids are heated through and the liquid is bubbly. Meanwhile, add the hottest possible tap water to an insulated vacuum bottle. Let stand for a few minutes to warm the bottle. Discard the water and transfer the hot food from the saucepan to the bottle. Seal tightly and carry in an insulated lunch box.

Restaurant Dining

Eating out is easier than ever for dieters. More and more restaurants are offering light or diet dishes on their menus. Here are some tips to help you stay on your diet when you eat out.

- If possible, select a restaurant that offers diet, light, or heart-healthy entrées. They're becoming more common.
- Most of the time, a restaurant serving will be larger than your diet plan allows. Don't eat the entire portion. Instead, ask for a doggie bag and save the rest for a later meal.
- When ordering a baked potato, ask for butter or sour cream on the side.
- When you order a salad, ask for a low-calorie dressing and request that it be served on the side.
- Many chain restaurants will provide nutritional information about their products on request. Several also have calculated Food Exchanges. Ask for this information when eating in these establishments.

Nutrition Analysis

	Per Serving									Percent U.S. RDA Per Serving							
	Servings (Per Recipe)	Calories	Protein (g)	Carbohydrate (g)	Total Fat (g)	Saturated Fat (g)	Cholesterol (mg)	Sodium (mg)	Potassium (mg)	Protein	Vitamin A	Vitamin C	Thiamine	Riboflavin	Niacin	Calcium	Iron
Athenian Lamb Kabobs (p. 65)	6	232	22	10	11	4	76	316	396	49	2	55	7	17	30	2	15
Baked Cajun Chicken (p. 20)	4	166	25	1	6	2	77	202	227	55	2	0	4	9	43	3	7
Barbecued Ham Slice (p. 59)	4	183	20	7	8	3	50	1277	438	43	1	51	44	18	27	1	7
Beef Burgundy (p. 52)	4	315	26	26	9	3	86	393	546	57	4	9	17	26	27	3	22
Beef Slaw-Wiches (p. 56)	4	238	21	18	9	2	57	384	347	47	3	37	11	12	17	5	18
Cajun Pork Pinwheels (p. 61)	3	230	24	3	13	5	81	244	441	53	3	30	50	19	26	2	8
Cheese-Stuffed Chicken Breasts (p. 25)	4	179	30	3	4	2	76	129	244	66	3	1	6	9	60	7	6
Chef's Salad Bowl (p. 63)	4	108	9	6	6	1	19	695	529	20	33	85	17	10	12	4	10
Chicken and Broccoli Skillet (p. 23)	4	186	28	5	6	1	72	77	449	63	20	79	8	10	61	4	9
Chicken Kabobs with Peanut Sauce (p. 28)	4	180	23	5	7	1	55	540	357	51	2	41	5	7	50	4	6
Chilled Poached Fish (p. 40)	4	120	20	7	2	1	33	218	548	45	6	40	6	6	2	12	3
Chinese Style Chicken (p. 21)	4	240	26	17	6	2	76	293	355	58	4	7	8	8	47	3	9
Country French Chicken (p. 20)	6	187	22	4	6	2	68	108	402	50	54	9	6	12	42	3	9
Easy Baked Fish (p. 40)	4	96	17	21	2	1	60	131	366	39	11	11	4	11	14	10	4
Eggs Florentine (p. 66)	4	208	13	25	6	2	214	553	555	29	65	14	13	30	11	16	14
Flounder Dijon (p. 36)	4	109	19	5	1	0	61	341	479	42	47	8	6	16	17	12	4
Fruited Chicken Salad (p. 35)	4	178	18	10	4	1	52	95	307	40	4	49	4	8	29	5	6
Fruited Crab Salad (p. 43)	3	149	14	15	4	1	61	269	671	32	27	60	5	8	3	14	9
Fruited Ham Toss (p. 64)	3	175	14	14	8	2	36	943	544	31	42	43	31	16	19	5	10
Garlic Chicken with Pasta (p. 31)	4	253	25	26	6	1	54	312	461	56	4	14	13	12	56	3	12
Garlic-Marinated Swordfish Steaks (p. 36)	4	147	22	3	5	1	80	196	442	49	2	5	4	11	19	6	3
Ham Burritos (p. 64)	2	191	16	19	5	1	19	689	183	36	3	22	16	16	14	9	10
Hearty Salmon Pie (p. 45)	6	334	28	29	11	3	56	1008	885	62	54	41	12	22	46	8	15
Hot Chicken Salad (p. 23)	4	136	20	9	2	1	48	223	673	45	80	85	8	12	42	10	15
Lamb Chops with Peaches (p. 64)	8	153	16	5	7	3	52	65	253	36	2	15	4	8	20	1	7
Lean Veal Parmesan (p. 58)	4	182	25	7	5	2	88	358	290	56	3	5	5	13	36	4	7
Lemon Chicken with Curried Rice (p. 26)	4	234	29	20	4	1	72	230	244	64	2	4	4	5	58	1	6
Lemon-Poached Halibut (p. 39)	4	158	22	7	5	1	84	341	497	50	42	13	5	13	19	9	4
Lime Beef-and-Chicken Kabobs (p. 50)	4	204	29	9	6	2	78	187	500	64	7	51	9	10	51	3	13
Mandarin Chicken Dinner (p. 34)	4	289	21	31	6	1	51	597	340	46	8	41	18	11	37	4	24
Mexican-Style Fish Fillets (p. 38)	4	200	25	19	2	0	41	304	632	56	22	19	10	3	7	6	6
Mustard-Marinated Steak (p. 49)	4	146	16	1	9	2	46	68	213	35	0	0	4	9	11	1	11
Old-Fashioned Beef Stew (p. 48)	4	236	20	31	4	1	42	451	818	45	291	30	13	13	26	5	16
One-Pot Spaghetti (p. 56)	7	283	19	27	12	5	46	762	622	42	14	42	13	13	23	9	18
Orange-Sauced Chicken Stir-Fry (p. 24)	4	283	25	31	7	1	54	323	662	56	30	191	16	13	53	7	12
Oriental Chicken Stir-Fry (p. 28)	2	268	30	24	6	1	72	250	537	67	100	15	12	8	65	4	11
Oriental Fish with Pasta (p. 39)	4	259	26	26	5	0	38	394	430	57	22	38	39	13	52	5	13
Oven-Fried Fish (p. 38)	4	147	23	5	3	1	80	263	424	51	1	1	4	12	20	6	4
Pasta Ham Salad (p. 61)	4	226	14	23	9	3	27	535	345	31	5	33	22	13	18	2	9
Pineapple and Pork Stir-Fry (p. 59)	4	207	19	25	3	1	59	349	573	42	2	63	44	14	17	2	9

Nutrition Analysis

	Per Serving									Percent U.S. RDA Per Serving							
	Servings (Per Recipe)	Calories	Protein (g)	Carbohydrate (g)	Total Fat (g)	Saturated Fat (g)	Cholesterol (mg)	Sodium (mg)	Potassium (mg)	Protein	Vitamin A	Vitamin C	Thiamine	Riboflavin	Niacin	Calcium	Iron
Plum-Chicken Stir-Fry (p. 29)	4	229	23	26	4	1	54	308	373	51	2	53	12	7	50	4	13
Poached Fish with Lime Sauce (p. 41)	4	132	24	5	2	0	82	243	483	52	4	3	5	16	19	13	4
Polynesian Shrimp (p. 44)	4	239	17	33	4	1	120	670	490	33	149	64	14	6	17	6	22
Pork Medaillons with Apple-Yogurt Sauce (p. 63)	4	267	24	32	5	2	63	218	610	53	1	6	45	23	20	10	11
Quick Chicken Cacciatore (p. 24)	4	178	27	7	3	1	72	328	443	61	7	24	7	11	63	4	10
Roast Beef with Mushroom Sauce (p. 48)	8	165	22	2	7	2	65	270	232	48	1	3	4	11	14	1	20
Round Steak Stroganoff (p. 53)	4	274	24	30	5	2	70	521	583	53	91	15	16	26	24	13	16
Salsa-Topped Frittata (p. 66)	3	131	14	6	6	3	84	531	314	31	7	21	4	23	7	2	6
Saucy Shrimp with Artichoke Hearts (p. 44)	6	163	15	21	1	0	107	333	217	33	1	4	10	6	12	8	20
Savory Steak and Gravy (p. 52)	4	150	22	4	4	1	55	167	377	50	0	5	8	17	23	1	13
Skillet Potato Dinner (p. 60)	4	253	22	25	7	3	40	1037	898	50	17	148	33	22	25	19	10
Smoked Turkey Salad (p. 34)	2	118	18	6	3	1	55	404	485	41	31	31	7	10	24	6	10
Spaghetti Squash with Tomato Sauce (p. 54)	6	232	18	15	11	4	48	415	1074	40	19	67	15	17	28	6	20
Spicy Baked Chicken (p. 21)	4	223	27	12	7	2	76	381	260	59	4	3	9	13	47	4	9
Spicy Marinated Pork Chops (p. 60)	4	267	23	17	11	4	71	247	468	51	7	39	48	17	28	2	9
Spinach-Topped Halibut (p. 41)	4	160	26	8	2	1	83	345	642	58	59	16	7	21	20	23	7
Steak with Marsala Sauce (p. 50)	4	188	21	3	8	3	61	168	410	48	2	7	8	17	19	2	16
Stir-Fried Beef and Spinach (p. 54)	4	172	19	8	7	2	43	349	820	48	74	44	9	17	19	7	22
Stir-Fried Scallops with Pasta (p. 43)	4	247	23	26	4	1	37	340	617	51	50	9	11	13	17	4	9
Sweet Pepper and Turkey Rolls (p. 30)	3	151	27	6	1	0	71	200	546	60	8	68	7	8	35	3	12
Taco Chicken Stew (p. 34)	4	274	25	33	5	1	51	801	603	56	17	84	20	13	40	8	22
Taco Compuesto (p. 53)	4	365	24	22	21	7	66	604	486	53	21	38	11	14	22	11	17
Tangy Salmon Salad (p. 45)	2	208	23	7	11	3	4	787	636	51	38	33	7	16	38	4	10
Teriyaki Chicken Kabobs (p. 31)	4	139	20	3	2	1	54	439	273	44	6	46	4	5	44	1	6
Tex-Mex Turkey Tenderloins (p. 26)	4	153	27	4	3	1	59	119	416	59	17	48	7	9	32	3	11
Tijuana Taco Salad (p. 49)	6	213	18	7	13	5	53	257	548	40	17	28	8	11	18	8	14
Tofu and Broccoli Stir-Fry (p. 65)	4	209	14	29	5	0	0	226	407	31	14	112	12	8	8	15	19
Tuna Bulgur Salad (p. 46)	4	193	15	20	6	1	18	443	326	33	8	21	6	3	13	2	9
Tuna Pockets (p. 46)	4	135	15	14	2	0	19	505	266	33	81	8	8	5	18	2	5
Tuna Toss (p. 45)	4	103	14	5	3	1	20	349	397	30	34	32	6	5	16	3	6
Turkey Loaf (p. 30)	4	274	23	16	12	3	60	235	108	51	2	17	4	5	3	3	4
Turkey Potpie (p. 33)	4	207	21	20	5	3	50	395	566	47	16	43	12	10	32	7	12
Turkey Waldorf Salad (p. 35)	2	229	15	26	9	2	44	541	607	33	6	81	10	16	19	10	10
Turkey Ham Pilaf (p. 33)	4	256	14	38	5	1	0	538	329	31	7	29	5	10	12	3	10
Veal and Peppers Italiano (p. 58)	4	338	36	31	7	2	139	409	720	80	11	92	15	21	55	6	21
Veal Chops with Vegetables (p. 57)	4	215	33	7	6	2	114	285	718	73	7	87	9	25	53	2	12
Veal Scallopini (p. 57)	4	164	18	3	7	3	65	215	339	40	1	3	6	19	25	1	14
Wine-Marinated Chicken (p. 29)	4	155	26	0	3	1	72	208	243	58	0	0	4	5	58	1	6

Side Dishes

Select your Vegetable and Starch/Bread Exchanges from these calorie-conscious vegetable, soup, and salad recipes. They add flavor, variety, and texture to your meals.

ASPARAGUS WITH DIJON SAUCE

Dress up your dinner menu with these asparagus spears and their creamy mustard sauce.

¾ pound asparagus spears *or* one 10-ounce package frozen asparagus spears
½ cup skim milk
2 teaspoons cornstarch
1 teaspoon Dijon-style mustard
   Dash white pepper
1 teaspoon grated Parmesan cheese

Snap off and discard the woody bases of the fresh asparagus. If desired, scrape off scales on stalks. Cook fresh asparagus, covered, in a small amount of boiling water for 8 to 10 minutes or till crisp-tender. (*Or,* cook frozen asparagus according to package directions.) Drain asparagus; transfer to a serving platter. Keep warm.

For sauce, in a small saucepan stir together milk and cornstarch. Cook and stir over medium heat till mixture is thickened and bubbly. Cook and stir for 2 minutes more. Stir in mustard and white pepper.

Spoon sauce atop asparagus. Sprinkle with Parmesan cheese. Makes 4 servings. One serving equals:

   ■ **Vegetable Exchange**

SAUTÉED PEPPERS AND TOMATOES

The garden-fresh flavor of this colorful combo complements any meat, fish, or poultry.

1 green pepper
2 cups cherry tomatoes
1 tablespoon snipped fresh basil *or* 1 teaspoon dried basil, crushed
2 teaspoons cooking oil
⅛ teaspoon garlic salt
⅛ teaspoon pepper

Cut green pepper in half lengthwise. Remove stem, seeds, and core from pepper. Cut pepper into thin strips; set aside.

Remove stems from cherry tomatoes. Cut in half; set aside.

In a large skillet, cook green pepper strips and basil in hot oil for 3 minutes. Add cherry tomatoes. Cover and cook for 1 to 2 minutes more or till heated through. Sprinkle with garlic salt and pepper. Makes 4 (¾-cup) servings. One serving equals:

   ■ **Vegetable Exchange**
   ■ **Fat Exchange**

CAULIFLOWER-ASPARAGUS STIR-FRY

When buying fresh asparagus, choose slender stalks. They'll be more tender than thicker stalks.

¾ **pound asparagus spears** *or* **one 10-ounce package frozen cut asparagus, thawed and drained**
¼ **cup chicken broth**
1 **teaspoon cornstarch**
¼ **teaspoon ground ginger**
¼ **teaspoon finely shredded lemon peel**
⅛ **teaspoon garlic powder**
Nonstick spray coating
1½ **cups thinly sliced cauliflower flowerets**

Snap off and discard the woody bases of the fresh asparagus. If desired, scrape off scales on stalks. Bias-slice asparagus into 1- or 2-inch pieces. Set aside.

For sauce, stir together chicken broth, cornstarch, ginger, lemon peel, and garlic powder. Set aside.

Spray a *cold* large skillet or wok with nonstick coating. Preheat wok or skillet over medium heat. Add cauliflower; stir-fry for 1 minute. Add asparagus; stir-fry for 3 to 4 minutes or till cauliflower and asparagus are crisp-tender. Push vegetables from center of wok or skillet.

Stir sauce; add to the center of the wok or skillet. Cook and stir till mixture is thickened and bubbly. Cook and stir for 2 minutes more. Stir all the ingredients together to coat with sauce. Makes 4 (¾-cup) servings. One serving equals:

■ ■ **Vegetable Exchanges**

Break the cauliflower head into flowerets. Then, thinly slice flowerets with a sharp knife.

GREEN BEANS AND WATER CHESTNUTS

A quick fix-up for frozen green beans.

½ **of an 8-ounce can sliced water chestnuts, drained**
1 **9-ounce package frozen French-style green beans**
1 **tablespoon soy sauce**
⅛ **teaspoon garlic powder**
⅛ **teaspoon ground ginger**

If desired, cut water chestnut slices in half. In a medium saucepan cook green beans according to package directions, adding the water chestnuts. Drain; return hot green beans and water chestnuts to pan.

Stir together soy sauce, garlic powder, and ground ginger. Add to green bean mixture; toss to coat. Makes 4 (½-cup) servings. One serving equals:

■ **Vegetable Exchange**

VEGETABLE-PASTA SALAD

Oil-free salad dressing adds lots of flavor, but few calories, to this tasty salad.

2 ounces corkscrew macaroni
1 10-ounce package frozen cut broccoli, thawed and drained, *or* 2 cups sliced, halved zucchini
1 cup chopped, seeded tomato
2 tablespoons sliced green onion
⅓ cup oil-free Italian salad dressing
¼ cup sliced radishes
2 cups torn lettuce

Cook macaroni according to package directions. Drain. Rinse with cold water.

In a large mixing bowl combine macaroni, broccoli or zucchini, tomato, and green onion. Add salad dressing; toss to coat. Cover and chill for 2 to 24 hours.

To serve, stir sliced radishes into the macaroni mixture. Serve over torn lettuce. Makes 4 (1-cup) servings. One serving equals:

▌ Starch/Bread Exchange
▌ Vegetable Exchange
▌ Fat Exchange

CREAMY VEGETABLE TOSS

A colorful salad to brighten your meal.

1 9-ounce package frozen Italian-style green beans
1 cup sliced, halved yellow summer squash *or* zucchini
1 cup sliced fresh mushrooms
¼ cup chopped sweet red *or* green pepper
1 tablespoon sliced green onion
½ teaspoon dried basil, crushed
¼ cup reduced-calorie buttermilk salad dressing
4 lettuce leaves

Cook the frozen Italian-style green beans according to package directions. Rinse; drain.

In a large mixing bowl combine green beans, summer squash or zucchini, mushrooms, sweet red or green pepper, and green onion.

Stir basil into buttermilk salad dressing. Add dressing to vegetable mixture; toss to coat. Cover and chill for 4 to 24 hours. Serve on lettuce leaves. Makes 4 (¾-cup) servings. One serving equals:

▌ Vegetable Exchange
▌ Fat Exchange

Vegetable-
Pasta Salad

CALORIE-COUNTER'S COLESLAW

Use the coarse blade of your vegetable shredder to shred the cabbage and the carrot.

2 cups shredded cabbage
¾ cup shredded carrot
2 tablespoons finely chopped onion
½ cup plain low-fat yogurt
1 tablespoon reduced-calorie mayonnaise
    or salad dressing
½ teaspoon prepared mustard
⅛ teaspoon salt
⅛ teaspoon celery seed
    Dash pepper

In a medium mixing bowl combine cabbage, carrot, and onion. Set aside.

For dressing, stir together yogurt, mayonnaise or salad dressing, mustard, salt, celery seed, and pepper. Mix well.

Add dressing to cabbage mixture; toss to coat vegetables with dressing. Cover and chill for 1 to 24 hours. Makes 4 (¾-cup) servings. One serving equals:

▌ **Vegetable Exchange**
▌ **Fat Exchange**

POTLUCK POTATO SALAD

Tote this tangy potato salad to your next potluck supper. No one will guess it's low in calories.

5 medium potatoes (1¾ pounds)
¼ cup low-calorie French salad dressing
1 cup chopped celery
½ cup chopped green pepper
⅓ cup chopped onion
¼ cup sliced radishes
½ cup reduced-calorie mayonnaise *or*
    salad dressing
2 teaspoons prepared mustard
1 teaspoon celery seed
½ teaspoon salt
½ to 1 teaspoon prepared horseradish
    (optional)

In a covered large saucepan cook potatoes in boiling salted water for 20 to 25 minutes or till just tender; drain well. Cool slightly. Peel and cube potatoes.

In a large mixing bowl combine warm potatoes and French salad dressing; toss gently to coat. Cover and chill for 2 hours.

Add celery, green pepper, onion, and radishes to the potato mixture.

For dressing, combine reduced-calorie mayonnaise or salad dressing, mustard, celery seed, salt, and, if desired, horseradish; mix well. Add dressing to the potato mixture; toss gently. Chill for 4 to 24 hours. Makes 8 (⅔-cup) servings. One serving equals:

■ **Starch/Bread Exchange**
▌■ **Fat Exchanges**

SPINACH SALAD

A lime-and-sesame dressing coats spinach, mushrooms, radishes, and slices of hard-cooked egg.

2 tablespoons salad oil
¼ teaspoon finely shredded lime peel
4 teaspoons lime juice
1 teaspoon sesame seed, toasted
¼ teaspoon dry mustard
⅛ teaspoon salt
3 cups torn fresh spinach
1 cup sliced fresh mushrooms
½ cup sliced radishes
1 hard-cooked egg, sliced

For dressing, in a screw-top jar combine salad oil, lime peel, lime juice, sesame seed, mustard, and salt. Cover; shake well.

For salad, in a salad bowl combine spinach, mushrooms, radishes, and egg. Shake dressing well. Add dressing to salad; toss. Makes 6 (1-cup) servings. One serving equals:

Vegetable Exchange
Fat Exchange

ZESTY TOMATO SALAD DRESSING

Doubles as a tasty sauce for seafood.

½ cup tomato juice
1 teaspoon cornstarch
2 tablespoons plain low-fat yogurt
2 tablespoons chili sauce
1½ teaspoons lemon juice
1 teaspoon prepared horseradish
1 teaspoon sweet pickle relish

In a small saucepan stir together tomato juice and cornstarch. Cook and stir over medium heat till mixture is thickened and bubbly. Cook and stir for 2 minutes more. Remove from heat. Stir in yogurt, chili sauce, lemon juice, horseradish, and relish. Cover and chill till serving time. Makes 6 (2-tablespoon) servings. One serving equals:

Free Exchange

BLUE CHEESE DRESSING

Cottage cheese makes the dressing creamy, but keeps the fat content low.

½ cup low-fat cottage cheese
2 tablespoons crumbled blue cheese
2 teaspoons lemon juice
Dash pepper
¼ cup skim milk

In a blender container combine cottage cheese, blue cheese, lemon juice, and pepper. Cover; blend till smooth. Add milk, 1 tablespoon at a time, blending well after each addition. (Dressing will thicken while chilling.) Transfer dressing to a small bowl. Cover; chill till serving time. Makes 6 (2-tablespoon) servings. One serving equals:

Lean Meat Exchange

SWEET-AND-SOUR SESAME DRESSING

Serve this fruity dressing over a salad of mixed greens and bean sprouts.

1 teaspoon cornstarch
⅛ teaspoon garlic powder
⅛ teaspoon ground ginger
1 5½-ounce can (⅔ cup) apricot nectar
3 tablespoons red wine vinegar
½ teaspoon sesame oil

In a small saucepan combine cornstarch, garlic powder, and ginger. Stir in apricot nectar. Cook and stir over medium heat till mixture is thickened and bubbly. Cook and stir for 2 minutes more. Remove from heat. Stir in red wine vinegar and sesame oil. Cover and chill at least 30 minutes before serving. Makes 6 (2-tablespoon) servings. One serving equals:

Free Exchange

Onion Soup
Parmesan

ONION SOUP PARMESAN

The flavor of the soup gets a boost from shredded fresh Parmesan cheese.

4 ounces French bread
1 cup thinly sliced onions
4 teaspoons instant beef bouillon granules
½ teaspoon Worcestershire sauce
2 tablespoons dry sherry
2 tablespoons finely shredded fresh Parmesan cheese

For croutons, cut French bread into 1-inch cubes. Place cubes on a baking sheet. Bake in a 350° oven for 10 to 15 minutes or till cubes are dry and crisp. Set aside.

In a large saucepan combine sliced onions, beef bouillon granules, Worcestershire sauce, 3½ cups *water*, and dash *pepper*. Bring to boiling; reduce heat. Cover and simmer about 20 minutes or till the onions are very tender. Stir in dry sherry. Ladle soup into bowls or cups. Pass croutons and finely shredded fresh Parmesan cheese to sprinkle atop soup. Makes 4 (1-cup) servings. One serving equals:

- ■ Starch/Bread Exchange
- ▌ Vegetable Exchange

CUCUMBER-BUTTERMILK SOUP

Serve this refreshing soup icy cold.

2 cups buttermilk
½ cup shredded seeded cucumber
1 tablespoon snipped parsley
1 tablespoon sliced green onion
½ teaspoon instant chicken bouillon granules
½ teaspoon dried dillweed

Combine buttermilk, cucumber, parsley, onion, bouillon granules, dillweed, and a dash *pepper*. Cover; chill 3 to 24 hours. Makes 2 (1-cup) servings. One serving equals:

- ▊ Milk Exchange
- ▌ Fat Exchange

CORN-CLAM CHOWDER

Corn replaces potatoes in our speedy version of New England clam chowder.

1 cup frozen mixed vegetables
¾ cup water
¼ cup chopped onion
¼ cup sliced celery
¼ cup chopped green pepper
1 clove garlic, minced
1½ teaspoons instant chicken bouillon granules
¼ teaspoon dried thyme, crushed
1 13-ounce can (1⅔ cups) evaporated skim milk
4 teaspoons cornstarch
1 8-ounce can whole kernel corn, drained
1 6½-ounce can minced clams

In a medium saucepan combine frozen mixed vegetables, water, onion, celery, green pepper, garlic, bouillon granules, and thyme. Bring to boiling; reduce heat. Cover and simmer for 8 to 10 minutes or till vegetables are just tender.

Stir together evaporated skim milk and cornstarch. Stir into hot vegetable mixture. Cook and stir over medium heat till mixture is thickened and bubbly. Cook and stir for 2 minutes more. Stir in corn and *undrained* clams. Heat through. Makes 4 (1-cup) servings. One serving equals:

- ▌ Lean Meat Exchange
- ■ Starch/Bread Exchange
- ▌ Vegetable Exchange
- ▊ Milk Exchange

CREAMY ASPARAGUS SOUP

Makes a delicious first-course soup.

2 cups asparagus cut into 1-inch pieces *or* one 10-ounce package frozen cut asparagus
1 medium onion, quartered
½ cup water
4 teaspoons instant chicken bouillon granules
½ teaspoon finely shredded lemon peel
⅛ teaspoon pepper
3 cups skim milk
2 tablespoons cornstarch

In a large saucepan combine fresh or frozen asparagus, onion, water, bouillon granules, lemon peel, and pepper. Bring to boiling; reduce heat. Cover and simmer for 7 to 9 minutes (for frozen asparagus, simmer about 5 minutes) or till asparagus is tender.

Transfer *half* of the asparagus mixture to a blender container or food processor bowl. Cover and blend or process till mixture is smooth. Pour into bowl. Repeat with the remaining asparagus mixture.

Return all of the asparagus mixture to the saucepan. Stir together milk and cornstarch; add to asparagus mixture. Cook and stir over medium heat till thickened and bubbly. Cook and stir for 2 minutes more. Makes 6 (¾-cup) servings. One serving equals:

■ **Vegetable Exchange**
▮ **Milk Exchange**

HERBED TOMATO SOUP

Freeze any leftovers in individual portions. Reheat in your microwave oven for an easy snack.

Nonstick spray coating
½ **cup thinly sliced onion**
1¼ **cups water**
3 **medium tomatoes, peeled and quartered**
½ **of a 6-ounce can (⅓ cup) tomato paste**
1 **tablespoon snipped fresh basil *or* 1 teaspoon dried basil, crushed**
1 **tablespoon snipped fresh thyme *or* 1 teaspoon dried thyme, crushed**
1½ **teaspoons instant chicken bouillon granules**
¼ **teaspoon salt**
   Few dashes bottled hot pepper sauce
   Dash pepper
1 **tablespoon snipped parsley *or* chives (optional)**

Spray a *cold* large saucepan with nonstick coating. Preheat the saucepan over medium heat. Add onion; cook and stir till tender but not brown. Stir in water, tomatoes, tomato paste, basil, thyme, chicken bouillon granules, salt, hot pepper sauce, and pepper. Bring to boiling; reduce heat. Cover and simmer for 30 minutes.

Transfer about *half* of the tomato mixture to a blender container or food processor bowl. Cover and blend or process till smooth. (*Or*, press mixture through a food mill.) Repeat with remaining tomato mixture. Return all of the tomato mixture to the saucepan. Heat through. If desired, sprinkle with snipped parsley *or* chives. Makes 4 (¾-cup) servings. One serving equals:

■ ■ **Vegetable Exchanges**

CREAMY CARROT-POTATO BOATS

For a "free" garnish, chop the tops of the green onions and sprinkle over the potato boats before serving.

4 **small baking potatoes (3 to 4 ounces each)**
1 **8-ounce can sliced *or* diced carrots, drained**
½ **of an 8-ounce container reduced-calorie soft-style cream cheese**
1 **to 2 tablespoons skim milk**
⅛ **teaspoon pepper**
2 **tablespoons chopped green onions**

Bake potatoes in a 375° oven about 45 minutes or till tender. Cool slightly.

Cut potatoes in half lengthwise. Gently scoop out each potato half, leaving a thin shell. In a small mixer bowl combine potato pulp, carrots, cream cheese, *1 tablespoon* milk, and pepper. Beat till smooth, adding more milk, if necessary. Stir in green onions.

Spoon potato mixture into potato shells. Place on a baking sheet. Bake in a 375° oven for 15 to 18 minutes or till heated through. Makes 8 servings. One serving equals:

■ ■ **Starch/Bread Exchanges**
　▏ **Vegetable Exchange**

Use a spoon to scoop out the inside of each potato half, leaving a shell about ⅛ inch thick.

To refill the potato halves, spoon the carrot-potato mixture into the shells.

SLENDER FRENCH FRIES

Just as crispy and delicious as traditional French fries, but much lower in calories and fat.

    2 medium potatoes (12 ounces total)
    2 teaspoons cooking oil
    ¼ teaspoon paprika
    ⅛ teaspoon salt
    ¼ cup catsup (optional)

Cut potatoes lengthwise into ½-inch sticks. Place strips in a bowl of ice water to crisp. Drain; pat dry with paper towels.

Place potato strips in a plastic bag; add cooking oil, paprika, and salt. Shake to coat.

On a large baking sheet arrange the potato strips in a single layer. Bake in a 425° oven for 30 to 35 minutes or till golden, turning once or twice. If desired, serve with catsup. Makes 4 servings. One serving equals:

■ **Starch/Bread Exchange**
▌ **Fat Exchange**

WALDORF SALAD

A yogurt dressing reduces the calories in this traditional apple salad.

    1½ cups coarsely chopped apples
    ¼   cup chopped celery
    ¼   cup halved seedless red *or* green grapes
    ¼   cup plain low-fat yogurt
    2   tablespoons chopped walnuts
        Leaf lettuce (optional)

In a medium mixing bowl combine apples, celery, grapes, yogurt, and walnuts; mix well. Cover and chill for 2 to 24 hours. If desired, serve in a lettuce-lined bowl. Makes 4 (½-cup) servings. One serving equals:

▌ **Fruit Exchange**
▌ **Fat Exchange**

MARINATED TOMATOES AND CUCUMBERS

Another time, try this oil-free dill dressing on a tossed garden salad.

    1½ teaspoons snipped fresh dill *or*
          ½ teaspoon dried dillweed
    1   teaspoon regular powdered fruit pectin
    ¼   teaspoon garlic salt
    ⅛   teaspoon coarsely ground pepper
    ¼   cup water
    1   tablespoon white wine vinegar
    2   medium tomatoes, cut into wedges
    1¾ cups sliced cucumber
    ¼   cup sliced green onions
    4   lettuce leaves (optional)

For dressing, in a medium mixing bowl combine dill, pectin, garlic salt, and pepper. Stir in water and white wine vinegar.

Add tomatoes, cucumber, and green onions. Toss gently to coat vegetables with dressing. Cover and chill for 4 to 6 hours. If desired, serve on lettuce-lined plates. Makes 4 (1-cup) servings. One serving equals:

▌ **Vegetable Exchange**

TANGY VEGETABLE SALAD

Save time by buying cut-up vegetables from the salad bar or produce section in your grocery store.

⅔ cup cold water
2 teaspoons cornstarch
1 teaspoon Worcestershire sauce
½ teaspoon dry mustard
¼ teaspoon paprika
⅛ teaspoon salt
⅛ teaspoon garlic powder
3 tablespoons vinegar
3 tablespoons catsup
2 cups thinly sliced cauliflower flowerets, carrots, celery, *and/or* cucumbers
2 tablespoons sliced green onions
4 cups torn lettuce

For dressing, in a small saucepan stir together water, cornstarch, Worcestershire sauce, dry mustard, paprika, salt, and garlic powder. Cook and stir over medium heat till the mixture is thickened and bubbly. Cook and stir for 2 minutes more. Remove from heat. Stir in vinegar and catsup.

In a medium mixing bowl combine cauliflower, carrot, celery, and/or cucumber slices with green onions. Add dressing; toss to coat vegetables. Cover and chill for 2 to 24 hours, stirring occasionally.

To serve, place lettuce in a large salad bowl. Add vegetable mixture; toss to coat lettuce with the dressing. Makes 4 (1½-cup) servings. One serving equals:

■ **Vegetable Exchange**

VEGETABLE SKILLET

A medley of summertime vegetables stars in this fresh-tasting accompaniment.

Nonstick spray coating
2 cups sliced zucchini
½ cup chopped onion
½ cup shredded carrot
⅓ cup bias-sliced celery
¼ cup green pepper strips
¾ teaspoon snipped fresh basil *or*
    ¼ teaspoon dried basil, crushed
¼ teaspoon garlic salt
Dash pepper
1 tablespoon catsup
½ teaspoon prepared mustard
1 medium tomato, cut into 8 wedges

Spray a *cold* large skillet with nonstick coating. Preheat skillet over medium heat. Add zucchini, onion, carrot, celery, green pepper, basil, garlic salt, and pepper. Cook and stir for 2 to 3 minutes or till vegetables are just crisp-tender.

Stir together catsup and mustard; stir into vegetable mixture. Add tomato wedges; cook for 2 to 3 minutes or till heated through, stirring occasionally. Makes 4 (¾-cup) servings. One serving equals:

■ ■ **Vegetable Exchanges**

CARROTS AND PEA PODS IN ORANGE SAUCE

Serve this colorful vegetable combo with broiled chicken breasts or ham slices.

1 cup bias-sliced carrots
2 cups fresh pea pods *or* one 6-ounce package frozen pea pods
½ teaspoon finely shredded orange peel (set aside)
⅓ cup fresh *or* unsweetened orange juice
1 teaspoon cornstarch
2 teaspoons soy sauce

In a medium saucepan cook carrots in a small amount of boiling salted water, covered, for 5 minutes. Add fresh or frozen pea pods. Cook for 2 to 4 minutes more or till vegetables are crisp-tender. Drain; return to saucepan. Keep warm.

Meanwhile, for sauce, in a small saucepan combine orange juice and cornstarch. Cook and stir over medium heat till the mixture is thickened and bubbly. Cook and stir for 2 minutes more. Stir in orange peel and soy sauce. Pour sauce over vegetables. Toss vegetables with sauce. Makes 4 (½-cup) servings. One serving equals:

■ Starch/Bread Exchange
■ Vegetable Exchange

HERBED ZUCCHINI

We chose a sweet red pepper to brighten this dish, but green or yellow peppers taste just as good.

3 cups sliced zucchini *or* yellow summer squash (¼-inch-thick slices)
½ cup sweet red pepper strips
⅓ cup thinly sliced onion
¼ cup water
1½ teaspoons snipped fresh basil *or* ½ teaspoon dried basil, crushed
⅛ teaspoon garlic salt

In a medium saucepan combine zucchini or summer squash, red pepper, onion, and water. Bring to boiling; reduce heat. Cover and simmer about 5 minutes or till vegetables are crisp-tender. Drain. Sprinkle with basil and garlic salt; toss to mix. Makes 4 (¾-cup) servings. One serving equals:

■ Vegetable Exchange

HERBED MUSHROOMS

4 cups small fresh mushrooms
⅓ cup sliced onion
⅔ cup dry white wine
½ teaspoon dried basil, crushed
¼ teaspoon salt
⅛ teaspoon freshly ground pepper
1 tablespoon snipped parsley

Halve any large mushrooms. Separate onion into rings. In a large saucepan cook onion in small amount of boiling water for 1 minute. Add mushrooms and cook for 1 minute more. Drain; rinse with cold water. Set aside.

For marinade, in a small saucepan combine wine, basil, salt, and pepper. Bring to boiling; reduce heat. Simmer, uncovered, for 5 minutes. Remove from heat. Mix mushroom mixture and hot marinade. Cover; chill for 4 to 24 hours, stirring occasionally. Serve with a slotted spoon. Sprinkle with parsley. If desired, serve over lettuce leaves. Makes 6 (½-cup) servings. One serving equals:

■ Vegetable Exchange

Carrots and
Pea Pods in
Orange Sauce

SWEET POTATOES AND PINEAPPLE

Orange and pineapple juices sweeten the sauce.

3 medium sweet potatoes (1 pound total)
1 8-ounce can pineapple chunks (juice pack)
½ teaspoon finely shredded orange peel
   (set aside)
½ cup fresh *or* unsweetened orange juice
1 teaspoon cornstarch
¼ teaspoon ground cinnamon
   Dash ground nutmeg

In a large saucepan cook sweet potatoes, covered, in enough boiling water to cover for 25 to 35 minutes or till tender. Drain; cool slightly. Peel; cut into ¼-inch slices.

Drain pineapple, reserving juice. In a medium saucepan stir together reserved pineapple juice, orange juice, cornstarch, ground cinnamon, and ground nutmeg. Cook and stir over medium heat till the mixture is thickened and bubbly. Cook and stir for 2 minutes more. Stir in cooked sweet potatoes, pineapple chunks, and orange peel. Heat through. Makes 4 (¾-cup) servings. One serving equals:

  ▮ ▪ **Starch/Bread Exchanges**
   ▪ **Fruit Exchange**

BUTTERNUT SQUASH AND APPLES

This easy oven dish goes well with either a pork loin roast or baked ham.

½ cup unsweetened apple juice
2 tablespoons raisins
2 teaspoons quick-cooking tapioca, crushed
¼ teaspoon salt
¼ teaspoon ground nutmeg
   Dash ground cloves
3 cups cubed, peeled butternut squash
   (¾-inch pieces)
1 cup cubed apple (¾-inch pieces)

In a 1½-quart casserole stir together apple juice, raisins, tapioca, salt, nutmeg, and cloves. Let stand for 5 minutes.

Add butternut squash cubes and apple cubes to the tapioca mixture in the casserole; stir to coat. Bake, covered, in a 350° oven for 55 to 60 minutes or till the squash is tender, stirring once. Makes 4 (1-cup) servings. One serving equals:

  ▮ **Starch/Bread Exchange**
  ▪ **Fruit Exchange**

SAVORY BRAN MUFFINS

Parmesan cheese, chives, and Italian seasoning make these bran muffins out of the ordinary.

1½ cups all-purpose flour
 1 cup whole bran cereal
 2 tablespoons grated Parmesan cheese
 1 tablespoon snipped chives
 2 teaspoons baking powder
 ½ teaspoon salt
 ½ teaspoon dried Italian seasoning, crushed
 1 beaten egg
 1 cup skim milk
 ¼ cup cooking oil
    Nonstick spray coating

In a medium mixing bowl stir together all-purpose flour, whole bran cereal, Parmesan cheese, snipped chives, baking powder, salt, and Italian seasoning. Make a well in the center of the dry ingredients.

In a small mixing bowl combine egg, skim milk, and cooking oil. Add all at once to flour mixture. Stir just till moistened (batter should be lumpy).

Spray 12 muffin cups with nonstick coating. Divide batter evenly among muffin cups. Bake in a 400° oven about 20 minutes or till golden. Remove from pan; serve warm. Makes 12. One muffin equals:

■ Starch/Bread Exchange
▪ Fat Exchange

ORANGE-APPLESAUCE MUFFINS

A sugar-free muffin with a hint of cinnamon.

 2 cups all-purpose flour
1½ teaspoons baking powder
 ½ teaspoon baking soda
 ½ teaspoon ground cinnamon
 ¼ teaspoon salt
 1 beaten egg
 1 cup unsweetened applesauce
 1 teaspoon finely shredded orange peel
 ½ cup fresh *or* unsweetened orange juice
 3 tablespoons cooking oil
    Nonstick spray coating

In a medium mixing bowl combine all-purpose flour, baking powder, baking soda, ground cinnamon, and salt. Make a well in the center of the dry ingredients.

In a small mixing bowl combine egg, applesauce, orange peel, orange juice, and cooking oil. Add all at once to flour mixture. Stir just till moistened (batter should be lumpy).

Spray 12 muffin cups with nonstick coating. Divide batter evenly among muffin cups. Bake in a 400° oven about 20 minutes or till golden. Remove from pans; serve warm. Makes 12. One muffin equals:

■ Starch/Bread Exchange
▪ Fat Exchange

BULGUR AND VEGETABLES

This hearty pilaf uses bulgur instead of rice.

1 cup sliced fresh mushrooms
1 cup sliced, quartered zucchini
1 cup water
½ cup bulgur
⅓ cup chopped onion
⅓ cup shredded carrot
¼ cup chopped green pepper
1 clove garlic, minced
1 teaspoon instant chicken bouillon granules
½ teaspoon dried basil, crushed
¼ teaspoon celery seed
¼ teaspoon dried thyme *or* marjoram, crushed
 Dash pepper
½ cup chopped, seeded, peeled tomato

In a medium saucepan combine mushrooms, zucchini, water, bulgur, onion, carrot, green pepper, garlic, chicken bouillon granules, basil, celery seed, thyme or marjoram, and pepper. Bring to boiling; reduce heat. Cover and simmer for 5 minutes. Remove from heat; stir in chopped tomato.

Let stand, covered, for 5 minutes or till all the liquid is absorbed. Fluff the bulgur mixture with a fork. Makes 4 (¾-cup servings). One serving equals:

■ Starch/Bread Exchange
▪ Vegetable Exchange

CAJUN CORN AND OKRA

The vegetables and seasonings of Louisiana come to play in this spicy dish.

1 10-ounce package frozen whole kernel corn
1 10-ounce package frozen cut okra
⅓ cup water
¼ teaspoon salt
½ cup chopped, seeded, peeled tomato
¼ teaspoon onion powder
 Several dashes bottled hot pepper sauce

In a large saucepan combine corn, okra, water, and salt. Bring to boiling; reduce heat. Cover and simmer about 5 minutes or till vegetables are crisp-tender. Drain.

Stir in tomato, onion powder, and bottled hot pepper sauce. Heat through. Makes 4 (⅔-cup) servings. One serving equals:

■ Starch/Bread Exchange
▪ Vegetable Exchange

Cajun Corn and Okra

CURRIED ORANGE RICE

If you like spicy foods, use the larger amount of curry powder. For a milder taste, use the lesser amount.

1 cup water
1 teaspoon instant chicken bouillon
   granules
¼ to ½ teaspoon curry powder
⅓ cup long grain rice
1 medium orange
1 tablespoon sliced green onion
1 tablespoon snipped fresh parsley

In a medium saucepan combine water, chicken bouillon granules, and curry powder. Bring to boiling. Add uncooked rice. Return to boiling; reduce heat. Cover and simmer about 20 minutes or till rice is tender and liquid is absorbed.

Meanwhile, peel and section orange over a bowl to catch the juices. Cut up orange sections. Stir cut-up orange, juices, green onion, and parsley into the rice mixture. Heat through. Makes 3 (½-cup) servings. One serving equals:

■ Starch/Bread Exchange
▮ Fruit Exchange

WILD RICE AND MUSHROOMS

A delicious accompaniment for poultry or fish main dishes. (Pictured on the cover.)

¼ cup wild rice
   Nonstick spray coating
1 cup quartered fresh mushrooms
½ cup chopped onion
1 cup water
½ teaspoon instant beef *or* chicken
   bouillon granules
½ teaspoon dried sage, crushed
¼ teaspoon dried thyme, crushed
¼ cup brown rice

Rinse uncooked wild rice with cold water. Drain; set aside.

Spray a small saucepan with nonstick coating. Preheat the saucepan over medium heat. Add mushrooms and onion. Cook, stirring occasionally, till mushrooms and onion are tender.

Add water, beef or chicken bouillon granules, sage, and thyme. Bring to boiling. Add wild rice and uncooked brown rice. Return to boiling; reduce heat. Cover and simmer about 40 minutes or till wild rice and brown rice are tender. Makes 4 (½-cup) servings. One serving equals:

■ Starch/Bread Exchange
▮ Vegetable Exchange

HERBED RICE

Flecks of carrot, celery, and parsley color this versatile rice dish.

2 cups water
½ cup shredded carrot
½ cup sliced celery
⅓ cup chopped onion
2 teaspoons instant chicken bouillon
   granules
½ teaspoon dried marjoram, crushed
   Dash pepper
⅔ cup long grain rice
1 tablespoon snipped parsley

In a medium saucepan combine water, carrot, celery, onion, chicken bouillon granules, marjoram, and pepper. Bring to boiling.

Add uncooked rice to saucepan. Return to boiling; reduce heat. Cover and simmer about 20 minutes or till the rice is tender. Remove from heat. Let stand 5 minutes. Fluff with a fork. Stir in parsley. Makes 6 (½-cup) servings. One serving equals:

■ Starch/Bread Exchange
▌ Vegetable Exchange

PEPPER AND RICE TIMBALES

Impress the family and company with these easy-to-make rice molds.

1¼ cups water
1 teaspoon instant chicken bouillon
   granules
½ cup long grain rice
½ cup finely chopped green *or* sweet
   red pepper
   Nonstick spray coating

In a medium saucepan combine water and bouillon granules. Bring to boiling. Add uncooked rice. Return to boiling; reduce heat. Cover and simmer about 20 minutes or till rice is tender. Stir in chopped pepper. Cover; let stand for 10 minutes.

For each timbale, spray one 5-ounce custard cup or ½-cup measure with nonstick coating. Immediately pack *one-fourth* of the rice mixture into the custard cup or measure. Invert onto a serving plate. Remove custard cup or measure. Makes 4 (½-cup) servings. One serving equals:

■ Starch/Bread Exchange

Pack the rice into the custard cup and invert on the serving plate. Then, remove the custard cup.

Nutrition Analysis

	Servings (Per Recipe)	Calories	Protein (g)	Carbohydrate (g)	Total Fat (g)	Saturated Fat (g)	Cholesterol (mg)	Sodium (mg)	Potassium (mg)	Protein	Vitamin A	Vitamin C	Thiamine	Riboflavin	Niacin	Calcium	Iron
	Per Serving									**Percent U.S. RDA Per Serving**							
Asparagus with Dijon Sauce (p. 72)	4	43	4	7	1	0	1	46	238	9	15	35	4	8	5	7	3
Blue Cheese Dressing (p. 77)	6	28	3	1	1	1	3	121	42	7	1	1	1	3	0	4	0
Bulgur and Vegetables (p. 88)	4	104	3	23	1	0	0	224	307	7	36	24	8	7	10	2	10
Butternut Squash and Apples (p. 86)	4	86	1	22	0	0	0	138	390	2	89	29	5	2	5	4	5
Cajun Corn and Okra (p. 88)	4	83	4	20	0	0	0	142	356	9	9	27	9	5	8	4	3
Calorie-Counter's Coleslaw (p. 76)	4	50	2	7	2	0	3	110	252	5	118	40	4	5	2	8	2
Carrots and Pea Pods in Orange Sauce (p. 84)	4	61	3	13	0	0	0	201	286	6	194	92	10	5	4	5	10
Cauliflower-Asparagus Stir-Fry (p. 73)	4	38	4	7	1	0	0	58	334	8	14	80	6	7	7	3	4
Corn-Clam Chowder (p. 79)	4	176	14	30	2	0	32	651	544	31	72	24	11	23	9	31	18
Creamy Asparagus Soup (p. 80)	6	78	7	13	1	0	2	642	365	15	15	29	6	14	4	17	3
Creamy Carrot-Potato Boats (p. 81)	8	135	4	28	1	0	0	97	480	9	79	24	8	3	9	2	9
Creamy Vegetable Toss (p. 74)	4	50	2	8	2	0	2	55	260	4	13	27	6	9	6	5	6
Cucumber-Buttermilk Soup (p. 79)	2	106	9	13	2	1	9	475	439	19	6	11	6	23	1	30	3
Curried Orange Rice (p. 90)	3	98	2	22	0	0	0	292	117	4	3	42	8	2	4	2	7
Green Beans and Water Chestnuts (p. 73)	4	34	2	8	0	0	0	268	122	3	7	9	2	4	3	3	5
Herbed Mushrooms (p. 84)	6	33	1	3	0	0	0	107	225	2	1	5	3	11	10	1	4
Herbed Rice (p. 91)	6	85	2	19	0	0	0	304	100	4	33	5	6	1	4	1	7
Herbed Tomato Soup (p. 80)	4	47	2	10	1	0	0	636	440	5	32	45	7	6	7	3	10
Herbed Zucchini (p. 84)	4	22	1	4	0	0	0	67	286	3	8	36	6	2	2	4	4
Marinated Tomatoes and Cucumbers (p. 82)	4	21	1	5	0	0	0	135	214	2	19	25	4	3	3	2	3
Onion Soup Parmesan (p. 79)	4	116	5	18	2	1	3	1092	112	11	0	7	11	7	7	9	7
Orange-Applesauce Muffins (p. 87)	12	122	3	18	4	0	18	127	60	7	1	9	8	5	6	1	4
Pepper and Rice Timbales (p. 91)	4	88	2	19	0	0	0	219	43	4	1	20	7	1	4	1	7
Potluck Potato Salad (p. 76)	8	114	2	22	3	0	3	276	402	4	2	32	7	1	7	2	3
Sautéed Peppers and Tomatoes (p. 72)	4	37	1	4	3	0	0	69	156	1	14	55	3	2	2	1	4
Savory Bran Muffins (p. 87)	12	128	4	16	6	0	19	219	125	9	1	9	14	13	13	5	7
Slender French Fries (p. 82)	4	90	1	16	2	0	0	71	294	3	2	16	5	1	5	0	2
Spinach Salad (p. 77)	6	66	2	2	6	1	46	93	229	5	38	17	3	8	4	4	7
Sweet-and-Sour Sesame Dressing (p. 77)	6	21	0	5	0	0	0	1	32	0	7	0	0	0	0	0	1
Sweet Potatoes and Pineapple (p. 86)	4	139	2	34	0	0	0	10	430	4	234	70	8	6	4	3	4
Tangy Vegetable Salad (p. 83)	4	42	1	10	0	0	0	229	325	3	115	37	5	3	3	3	4
Vegetable-Pasta Salad (p. 74)	4	92	4	15	2	0	1	183	370	9	20	123	8	7	6	4	7
Vegetable Skillet (p. 83)	4	36	2	8	0	0	0	193	355	3	91	36	7	3	4	3	4
Waldorf Salad (p. 83)	4	61	2	9	3	0	1	17	133	4	1	5	2	3	1	3	1
Wild Rice and Mushrooms (p. 90)	4	89	2	19	1	0	0	111	100	4	0	4	2	4	4	1	2
Zesty Tomato Dressing (p. 77)	6	15	1	33	0	0	0	160	78	1	4	8	1	1	1	1	1

Desserts

If the terms "sweet" and "low-calorie" sound contradictory, take a look at this assortment of recipes that includes creamy *Apple Rice Pudding*, elegant *Melon Mousse*, and luscious *Mint-Chocolate Cream Puffs*.

CHERRY-BERRY COMPOTE

Add a twist of lemon peel for a calorie-free garnish.

1 tablespoon cornstarch
   Low-calorie granulated sugar substitute
   to equal 2 tablespoons sugar
2 teaspoons lemon juice
   Few drops almond extract
2 cups fresh strawberries *or* frozen unsweetened whole strawberries, thawed
3 cups fresh pitted dark sweet cherries,
   halved *or* one 16-ounce package frozen
   unsweetened pitted dark sweet
   cherries, thawed

For sauce, in a medium saucepan cook and stir cornstarch and ¾ cup *cold water* till thickened and bubbly. Cook and stir 2 minutes more. Remove from heat. Stir in sugar substitute, lemon juice, and almond extract.

Halve any large strawberries. Stir strawberries and cherries into sauce. Transfer to a bowl. Cover and chill 2 to 24 hours. Makes 8 (½-cup) servings. One serving equals:

■ Fruit Exchange

TROPICAL FRUIT CUP

1 8-ounce can pineapple chunks (juice pack)
1 large orange, peeled, sliced, and quartered
1 cup seedless grapes
3 ounces reduced-calorie cream cheese *or*
   Neufchâtel cheese, softened
   Ground nutmeg *or* cinnamon

Drain pineapple, reserving *3 tablespoons* of juice. Combine pineapple, orange, and grapes. Cover and chill. Meanwhile, mix cream cheese and reserved juice till smooth. Cover and chill. To serve, divide fruit mixture among *4* dessert dishes. Top *each* serving with *one-fourth* of the cream cheese mixture. Sprinkle with nutmeg. Makes 4 (1-cup) servings. One serving equals:

▪ Lean Meat Exchange
■ Fruit Exchange
▪ Fat Exchange

FRUITED COFFEE CAKE

2¼ to 2¾ cups all-purpose flour
  1 package active dry yeast
  ½ cup skim milk
  2 tablespoons sugar
  2 tablespoons margarine
  ½ teaspoon salt
  2 egg whites
    Nonstick spray coating
  ½ cup finely chopped, peeled peach *or* pear
  ⅓ cup reduced-calorie strawberry *or* rasp-
    berry preserves

In a large mixing bowl combine *1 cup* of the flour and the yeast. In a small saucepan heat and stir milk, sugar, margarine, and salt just till warm (115° to 120°). Add milk mixture and egg whites to flour mixture. Beat with an electric mixer on low speed for ½ minute, scraping bowl constantly. Beat on high speed for 3 minutes. Using a spoon, stir in as much of the remaining flour as you can.

On a lightly floured surface knead in enough of the remaining flour to make a moderately soft dough that is smooth and elastic (3 to 5 minutes total). Shape into a ball. Spray a bowl with nonstick coating. Add dough to bowl, turning once to coat. Cover; let rise in a warm place till double (about 1 hour).

Punch dough down. Cover; let rest for 10 minutes. Meanwhile, in a small bowl stir together chopped peach or pear, and preserves. On a lightly floured surface roll the dough into a 15x10-inch rectangle. Spread fruit mixture over dough. Roll up from one of the long sides. Pinch to seal. Spray a baking sheet with nonstick coating. Place roll, seam side down, on baking sheet. Bring ends together to form a ring; seal ends. At 1-inch intervals, cut into dough from outside edge to almost the center. Turn slices to one side. Cover; let rise in a warm place till nearly double (about 40 minutes). Bake in a 350° oven for 20 to 30 minutes or till golden. Remove from pan; cool on a wire rack. Makes 1 coffee cake (14 servings). One serving equals:

■ Starch/Bread Exchange
▪ Fat Exchange

ORANGE AND BERRY PARFAITS

This light dessert features fluffy orange layers and fresh raspberries or strawberries.

½ cup cold water
1 teaspoon unflavored gelatin
2 tablespoons frozen orange *or* pineapple juice concentrate
Low-calorie powdered sweetener to equal 1 tablespoon sugar
¼ cup ice water
1 tablespoon lemon juice
½ teaspoon vanilla
⅓ cup nonfat dry milk powder
1½ cup fresh raspberries, sliced fresh strawberries, *or* frozen unsweetened strawberries, thawed

In a small saucepan combine water and gelatin; let stand for 5 minutes. Add orange *or* pineapple juice concentrate. Cook and stir 6 to 8 minutes over medium heat or till mixture is boiling. Remove saucepan from heat.

Stir in low-calorie powdered sweetener; cool to room temperature.

Meanwhile, in a small mixing bowl combine ice water, lemon juice, and vanilla. Stir in dry milk powder. Beat with an electric mixer on high speed for 3 to 6 minutes or till soft peaks form. Fold into gelatin mixture.

In *6* parfait glasses alternately layer gelatin mixture and raspberries or strawberries. Chill for 6 to 24 hours. Makes 6 (½-cup) servings. One serving equals:

❚ **Fruit Exchange**

CHOCOLATE CHEESECAKE BARS

Tofu keeps the cheese layer creamy and reduces the fat in these delicious dessert squares.

Nonstick spray coating
¼ cup graham cracker crumbs
8 ounces tofu (bean curd), cut up
1 8-ounce package reduced-calorie cream cheese *or* Neufchâtel cheese, cut up
2 eggs
Non-caloric liquid sweetener to equal ½ cup sugar
¼ cup water
2 tablespoons unsweetened cocoa powder
2 teaspoons vanilla
2 tablespoons low-calorie strawberry, raspberry, *or* cherry preserves

Spray a 9x9x2-inch baking pan with nonstick coating. Sprinkle graham cracker crumbs over bottom of pan; set aside.

In a blender container or food processor bowl, combine tofu, cream cheese, eggs, non-caloric sweetener, water, cocoa powder, and vanilla. Cover and blend or process till smooth, stopping and scraping sides as necessary. Pour over crumbs in baking pan.

Bake in a 350° oven for 20 to 25 minutes or till set. Cool on rack.

In a small saucepan heat the preserves over low heat till melted. Drizzle melted preserves over bars. Makes 24 servings. One serving equals:

❚ **Lean Meat Exchange**
❚ **Fat Exchange**

Mint-
Chocolate
Cream Puffs

MINT-CHOCOLATE CREAM PUFFS

Both dieters and nondieters will revel in this delightful dessert.

Nonstick spray coating
½ cup water
2 tablespoons margarine
½ cup all-purpose flour
2 eggs
1 4-serving-size package reduced-calorie
    regular (not instant)
    vanilla pudding mix
2 tablespoons unsweetened cocoa powder
⅛ teaspoon peppermint extract
½ cup frozen whipped non-dairy dessert
    topping, thawed (optional)
    Ground nutmeg (optional)

Spray a baking sheet with nonstick coating; set aside. In a small saucepan combine water and margarine. Bring to boiling. Add flour all at once, stirring vigorously. Cook and stir till mixture forms a ball that doesn't separate. Remove from heat. Cool for 5 minutes. Add eggs one at a time, beating after each addition with a wooden spoon till mixture is shiny and smooth. Drop mixture in 8 mounds 3 inches apart on the baking sheet.

Bake in a 450° oven for 15 minutes. Reduce heat to 325°. Bake about 10 minutes or till golden. Turn oven off. Split puffs and remove any soft dough from inside. If desired, return cream puffs to oven for 20 minutes to dry. Cool on a wire rack.

For filling, in a medium saucepan combine vanilla pudding mix and cocoa powder. Prepare mix, according to package directions, *except* use skim milk. Stir in peppermint extract. Cover surface with waxed paper; chill.

To serve, spoon about *¼ cup* of the filling into the bottom half of *each* cream puff. If desired, top *each* with *1 tablespoon* whipped topping and sprinkle with nutmeg. Makes 8 servings. One serving equals:

▮ Starch/Bread Exchange
▮ Fat Exchange

MELON MOUSSE

This light and airy dessert is perfect for special occasions.

2 cups cubed honeydew melon, cantaloupe,
    Persian melon, casaba melon,
    or crenshaw melon
2 tablespoons melon *or* orange liqueur
    or orange juice
¼ cup water
1 envelope unflavored gelatin
⅓ cup frozen whipped nondairy dessert
    topping, thawed
    Mint leaves (optional)

In a blender container or food processor bowl combine cubed melon and liqueur or orange juice. Cover and blend or process till smooth. Set aside.

In a 1-cup glass measure or custard cup stir together water and gelatin. Let stand for 5 minutes.

In a small saucepan add water to the depth of 1 inch. Place the measure or custard cup containing the gelatin mixture in the water. Cook over medium heat, stirring gelatin mixture constantly, till the gelatin dissolves. Remove measure or cup from water.

In a medium mixing bowl combine pureed melon and gelatin mixture. Chill till partially set (consistency of unbeaten egg whites), stirring several times. Fold in the dessert topping. Pour into *four* ½-cup molds. Chill about 2 hours or till firm.

To serve, unmold onto serving plates. If desired, garnish with fresh mint leaves. Makes 4 (½-cup) servings. One serving equals:

▮ Fruit Exchange
▮ Fat Exchange

SUGAR SUBSTITUTES

For weight-conscious people, "low in calories" is a sweet message. Many people satisfy their sweet tooth by using low-calorie sweeteners instead of sugar. Because they have almost no calories, sugar substitutes added to coffee, tea, fruit, or breakfast cereals are Free Foods.

Two sugar substitutes, saccharin and aspartame, are commonly used. However, using them in cooking takes some know-how. Here are some tips for cooking with sugar substitutes:

- Add aspartame to recipes *after* cooking. Prolonged, high heat causes aspartame to lose its sweetness. Or use saccharin instead. Saccharin is much more stable when heated. Even then, you'll get the best results from saccharin-based sweeteners by adding them after cooking.
- With sugar substitutes, a little goes a long way. Check product labels to determine their sugar equivalent. The amount to use will vary from brand to brand.
- When you need the bulk that sugar provides, as in baked goods, use saccharin-based sweeteners for half, but not all, of the sugar. Even then, the baked item won't have the same volume it would if made with all sugar. Don't use aspartame because it has even less bulk and is not heat stable.
- Saccharin can leave a bitter aftertaste. Add a little fruit or fruit juice to help mask the flavor.
- If you need more guidance, order recipe brochures from sugar substitute manufacturers.

BERRY-SAUCED POACHED PEARS

Raspberries out of season? Use frozen, thawed ones instead. Rinse sweetened berries to remove sugar.

4 **small pears**
3 **cups water**
2 **tablespoons lemon juice**
1 **cup fresh raspberries**
½ **cup unsweetened pineapple juice**
2 **teaspoons cornstarch**
 Low-calorie powdered sweetener
  to equal 3 tablespoons sugar

Peel and core pears, leaving the stems intact. Cut a thin slice off the bottom of each pear so pears will stand upright.

In a large saucepan combine water and lemon juice. Bring to boiling. Add whole pears. Return to boiling; reduce heat. Cover and simmer for 10 to 15 minutes or till pears are tender, turning once. Transfer pears and cooking liquid to a medium mixing bowl. Cover and chill for 3 to 24 hours.

Meanwhile, for sauce, in a small saucepan combine raspberries, pineapple juice, and cornstarch. Cook and stir over medium heat till mixture is thickened and bubbly. Cook and stir for 2 minutes more. Press mixture through sieve to remove seeds; discard seeds. Transfer mixture to a bowl. Stir in sweetener. Cover and chill till serving time.

To serve, use a slotted spoon to lift pears from cooking liquid and place in dessert dishes. Spoon chilled sauce over pears. Makes 4 servings. One serving equals:

■ ■ ■ **Fruit Exchanges**

APPLE RICE PUDDING

Fool your taste buds. This naturally sweet dessert doesn't contain sugar or a sugar substitute.

 2   cups skim milk
 ½   teaspoon ground cinnamon
 ¼   teaspoon salt
     Dash ground nutmeg
 ⅓   cup long grain rice
1½   cups coarsely chopped apples
 ¼   cup frozen whipped nondairy dessert
        topping, thawed
     Ground nutmeg

In a heavy medium saucepan combine milk, cinnamon, salt, and nutmeg. Bring to boiling. Stir in uncooked rice. Cover and cook over low heat for 20 to 25 minutes or till most of the milk is absorbed, stirring occasionally. (Mixture may appear curdled.) Stir in chopped apples. Cool thoroughly.

Fold whipped dessert topping into the rice mixture. Spoon into 6 individual dessert dishes. Chill for 2 to 24 hours. If desired, sprinkle with additional ground nutmeg before serving. Makes 6 (½-cup) servings. One serving equals:

▮ **Starch/Bread Exchange**
▮ **Fruit Exchange**
▮ **Milk Exchange**
▮ **Fat Exchange**

BREAD PUDDING

A calorie-reduced version of a favorite dessert.

     Nonstick spray coating
 2   slices whole wheat bread, cubed (1½ cups)
 ¼   cup currants *or* raisins
 1   egg, beaten
 2   egg whites
 1   cup skim milk
 2   teaspoons vanilla
 ⅛   teaspoon ground nutmeg

Spray a 1-quart casserole with nonstick coating. Place bread cubes in the casserole. Sprinkle with currants or raisins. Set aside.

In a small mixing bowl beat together egg, egg whites, skim milk, vanilla, and nutmeg. Pour over bread and currants.

Bake in a 325° oven about 40 minutes or till a knife inserted near the center comes out clean. Cool slightly. Serve warm. Makes 4 (½-cup) servings. One serving equals:

▮ **Lean Meat Exchange**
▮ **Starch/Bread Exchange**
▮ **Fruit Exchange**

SUGAR SUBSTITUTES AND OUR RECIPES

Because different sugar substitutes react differently in cooking, each of our recipes specifies a particular substitute. Here's how we list the sweeteners in our recipes:

■ The term *low-calorie powdered sweetener* refers to an aspartame-based sweetener.
■ When a recipe calls for *low-calorie granulated sugar substitute* use a saccharin-based product.
■ Some recipes call for a liquid sweetener referred to as *non-caloric liquid sweetener.*

PEAR AND DATE CRISP

To reduce calories, a graham cracker crumb topping replaces the traditional brown sugar topping.

2 medium pears, peeled, cored, and sliced
5 pitted dates, snipped
1 tablespoon all-purpose flour
¼ cup frozen unsweetened apple juice concentrate, thawed
2 tablespoons water
½ teaspoon vanilla
¼ cup coarsely crushed graham crackers (2 crackers)
1 tablespoon all-purpose flour
¼ teaspoon ground cinnamon
2 tablespoons margarine

In a 1-quart casserole toss together pears and dates. Sprinkle with 1 tablespoon flour; toss to coat. Stir together apple juice concentrate, water, and vanilla. Drizzle over pear mixture. Cover casserole with lid or foil. Bake in a 375° oven for 25 to 30 minutes or till pears are tender.

In a small mixing bowl combine graham crackers, 1 tablespoon flour, and cinnamon. Cut in margarine till crumbly.

Remove lid from casserole. Sprinkle crumb mixture evenly over fruit. Bake, uncovered, for 5 to 10 minutes more or till topping is golden. Cool slightly. Serve warm. Makes 4 (⅔-cup) servings. One serving equals:

▮ Starch/Bread Exchange
▮ ▮ Fruit Exchanges
▮ ▮ Fat Exchanges

FRESH FRUIT PLATE

A delicious way to dress up fruit.

¼ cup reduced-calorie soft-style cream cheese
½ of an 8-ounce carton plain nonfat yogurt
1 tablespoon frozen orange juice concentrate
¼ teaspoon vanilla
4 cups sliced strawberries; sliced, peeled kiwi fruit; *and/or* raspberries
Mint leaves (optional)

In a small mixing bowl stir cream cheese till smooth. Add yogurt, juice concentrate, and vanilla; mix well. On *each* of four dessert plates, drizzle *one-fourth* of the cream cheese mixture. Arrange *1 cup* of fruit on each plate. If desired, garnish with mint leaves. Makes 4 servings. One serving equals:

▮ Fruit Exchange

APRICOT AND BANANA SHERBET

If you use the electric mixer method, you'll have slightly less volume, so allow ⅓ cup per serving.

1 ripe large banana
1 10-ounce jar apricot *or* strawberry all-fruit spread
Few drops food coloring (optional)
2½ cups buttermilk

Mash the banana. Stir in all-fruit spread, and if desired, food coloring. Stir in buttermilk. Freeze in a 2½-quart ice cream freezer according to manufacturer's directions. (*Or,* freeze in a 9x5x3-inch loaf pan about 4 hours or till firm. Break into chunks; place in a chilled mixing bowl. Beat with an electric mixer till smooth but not melted. Return to pan. Cover; freeze about 6 hours or till firm.) If necessary, let stand at room temperature about 10 minutes before serving. Makes 10 (½-cup) servings. One serving equals:

▮ Fruit Exchange

Fresh
Fruit Plate

FRESH FRUIT MEDLEY

Another time, serve this fruit trio as a salad.

½ of an 8-ounce container reduced-calorie
  soft-style cream cheese
1 8-ounce carton plain nonfat yogurt
  Non-caloric liquid sweetener to equal
  1 tablespoon sugar
2 ripe small bananas
2¼ cups fresh whole strawberries, halved
2 small oranges, peeled and sectioned

For sauce, in a small mixing bowl stir cream cheese till smooth. Add *half* of the yogurt; beat with a wooden spoon till smooth. Stir in remaining yogurt and liquid sweetener; mix well. Cover and chill till serving time.

Peel and bias-slice bananas. Gently mix sliced bananas, halved strawberries, and orange sections. Divide fruit among *8* dessert dishes. Spoon about *2 tablespoons* of sauce atop the fruit in *each* dish. Makes 8 (½-cup) servings. One serving equals:

■ Fruit Exchange

PUMPKIN CHIFFON PUDDING

Spicy in flavor, fluffy in texture, and low in calories.

¼ cup water
1 teaspoon unflavored gelatin
⅔ cup canned pumpkin
½ cup evaporated skim milk
  Low-calorie sweetener to equal
  2 tablespoons sugar
½ teaspoon pumpkin pie spice
½ cup frozen whipped nondairy dessert
  topping, thawed

In a small saucepan combine water and gelatin. Let stand for 5 minutes. Cook and stir over low heat till gelatin dissolves. Transfer to a medium mixing bowl. Stir in pumpkin, milk, sweetener, and pumpkin pie spice. Chill till partially set (the consistency of unbeaten egg whites). Fold in whipped topping. Spoon into individual dessert dishes. Chill for 1 to 3 hours or till firm. Makes 4 (⅓-cup) servings. One serving equals:

▌ Milk Exchange
■ Fat Exchange

Nutrition Analysis

	Servings (Per Recipe)	Calories	Protein (g)	Carbohydrate (g)	Total Fat (g)	Saturated Fat (g)	Cholesterol (mg)	Sodium (mg)	Potassium (mg)	Protein	Vitamin A	Vitamin C	Thiamine	Riboflavin	Niacin	Calcium	Iron
										Percent U.S. RDA Per Serving							
Apple Rice Pudding (p. 99)	6	97	4	18	1	1	1	132	186	8	4	5	5	7	2	11	4
Apricot and Banana Sherbet (p. 100)	10	73	2	15	1	0	2	91	138	5	1	3	2	6	0	7	0
Berry-Sauced Poached Pears (p. 98)	4	141	1	36	1	0	0	11	310	2	2	35	4	6	3	4	4
Bread Pudding (p. 99)	4	118	7	18	2	1	54	165	234	16	4	1	6	15	3	10	5
Cherry-Berry Compote (p. 94)	8	59	1	15	0	0	0	3	186	2	3	39	2	4	2	2	3
Chocolate Cheesecake Bars (p. 95)	24	66	3	4	4	2	25	59	59	7	2	0	1	3	1	2	7
Fresh Fruit Plate (p. 100)	4	85	4	15	2	0	1	44	343	9	1	149	4	10	2	8	3
Fresh Fruit Medley (p. 102)	8	88	4	16	1	0	1	43	314	9	2	73	4	8	2	8	2
Fruited Coffee Cake (p. 94)	14	106	3	19	2	0	0	117	56	7	2	0	9	8	6	2	3
Melon Mousse (p. 97)	4	59	2	10	2	1	0	13	290	4	2	41	5	1	3	1	1
Mint-Chocolate Cream Puffs (p. 97)	8	124	5	12	6	2	53	239	38	10	6	0	5	11	2	9	3
Orange and Berry Parfaits (p. 95)	6	42	3	8	0	0	1	24	181	7	2	33	2	5	1	4	2
Pear and Date Crisp (p. 100)	4	185	1	33	6	1	0	88	268	3	5	6	4	5	3	2	4
Pumpkin Chiffon Pudding (p. 102)	4	79	4	10	3	2	1	47	240	10	184	5	2	7	1	11	5
Tropical Fruit Cup (p. 94)	4	124	3	18	5	3	17	87	204	6	7	41	7	5	2	4	2

Snacks

Work these slimming snacks into
your Daily Menu Plan.
Choose a refreshing beverage, a
zesty dip for vegetables,
or a calorie-trimmed pizza.

SNACKS

FRUIT AND YOGURT SHAKE

In testing, we discovered that if we added a little vanilla to this shake, we didn't need a sweetener.

1 8-ounce can peach halves (juice pack)
½ ripe small banana
½ cup plain nonfat yogurt
½ teaspoon vanilla
1 cup ice cubes

In a blender container combine *undrained* peaches, banana, yogurt, and vanilla. Cover and blend till smooth. Add ice cubes; cover and blend till frothy. Makes 2 (1¼-cup) servings. One serving equals:

■ Fruit Exchange
▌ Milk Exchange

You Can Fit Snacks Into Your Diet Plan

Is snacking OK? Yes, as long as your snacks fit into your Daily Menu Plan. Properly managed, snacks can take the edge off your appetite and keep you from overeating at meals.

Daily Menu Plans are planned for breakfast, lunch, and dinner. But there's nothing sacred about having only three meals per day. To help control your hunger pangs, you might spread your Food Exchanges out into four, five, or six mini-meals.

You may save a few Food Exchanges for a coffee break, a bedtime snack, or any other time you need a nutritional lift. Just keep track of the snacks you eat. It's easy to forget a not-so-innocent handful of peanuts or the buttered popcorn you ate at the movie theater.

Celery, cucumbers, and zucchini are nutritious snacks that are on the Free Foods list. Because they have less than 20 calories per serving, you can eat them without feeling guilty. Sugar-free hard candy, low-calorie soft drinks, coffee, and tea are also Free Foods, but they don't provide any nutrients.

MEXICAN-STYLE HOT CHOCOLATE

For a stronger cinnamon flavor, serve with a cinnamon stick stirrer.

2¾ cup nonfat dry milk powder
½ cup unsweetened cocoa powder
   Low-calorie granulated sugar substitute to equal ½ cup sugar
1 teaspoon ground cinnamon

For cocoa mix, in a storage container combine dry milk powder, cocoa powder, sugar substitute, and cinnamon. Mix well. Cover and store in a cool, dry place up to 8 weeks.

For each serving, place ⅓ cup of the cocoa mix in a mug. Add ⅔ cup boiling water; stir to mix. Makes 9 (8-ounce) servings. One serving equals:

   ▓ Milk Exchange
   ▌ Fat Exchange

HERBED TOMATO JUICE

Keep a pitcher of this flavorful beverage in the fridge. Serve it cold or heat it in your microwave oven.

2½ cups tomato juice
1 14½-ounce can beef broth
1 tablespoon lemon juice
1 teaspoon Worcestershire sauce
¼ teaspoon dried basil, crushed
¼ teaspoon dried thyme, crushed
6 thin lemon slices (optional)

In a medium saucepan combine tomato juice, beef broth, lemon juice, Worcestershire sauce, basil, and thyme. Bring to boiling; reduce heat. Cover and simmer for 5 minutes. Serve in mugs. Or, chill in a covered container and serve over ice cubes. If desired, garnish each serving with a thin lemon slice. Makes 6 servings. One serving (⅔ cup) equals:

   ▌ Vegetable Exchange

LOW-CALORIE THIRST QUENCHERS

For a refreshing snack enjoy a delicious fruit juice spritzer. To mix a spritzer, pour ½ cup of chilled *low-calorie cranberry juice cocktail, grapefruit juice, orange juice, or pineapple juice* into a glass. Add ⅓ cup chilled *carbonated water* and as many ice cubes as you like. Count as one Fruit Exchange.

Veggie
Pita Pizzas

VEGGIE PITA PIZZAS

For the topping, use leftover vegetables or cook up some frozen loose-pack mixed vegetables.

2 **6-inch pita bread rounds**
½ **of an 8-ounce can (½ cup) herbed *or* plain tomato sauce**
1 **cup cooked vegetable such as broccoli, mushrooms, cauliflower, green pepper, asparagus, *or* green beans**
½ **cup shredded part-skim mozzarella cheese (2 ounces)**

Split each pita bread round horizontally so you have four rounds. Place rounds on a baking sheet. Bake in a 450° oven for 2 to 3 minutes or till dry and crisp.

Spread each round with tomato sauce. Arrange vegetable on top of each round. Sprinkle with mozzarella cheese.

Bake in a 450° oven about 5 minutes or till cheese melts and pizzas are heated through. Makes 4 servings. One serving equals:

   Lean Meat Exchange
▮ **Starch/Bread Exchange**
   Vegetable Exchange
▮ **Fat Exchange**

SALMON-TOPPED PITA WEDGES

In a hurry? Skip the pita wedges and spread the salmon mixture on saltines or other low-fat crackers.

1 **6½-ounce can skinless, boneless salmon, drained and flaked**
¼ **cup finely chopped celery**
2 **tablespoons finely chopped green onion**
2 **tablespoons plain low-fat yogurt**
1 **tablespoon Dijon-style mustard**
1½ **teaspoon snipped fresh dill *or***
    ½ teaspoon dried dillweed
   Nonstick spray coating
2 **6-inch pita bread rounds**
4 **lettuce leaves**

In a medium mixing bowl combine salmon, celery, green onion, yogurt, mustard, and dill. Mix well. Spray a 1-cup mold or bowl, or a 10-ounce custard cup with nonstick coating. Press salmon mixture into the mold, bowl, or custard cup. Cover and chill for 2 to 24 hours.

For pita wedges, split each pita bread round horizontally so you have four rounds. Cut each round into 8 wedges. Arrange wedges on a baking sheet. Bake in a 450° oven for 2 to 3 minutes or till dry and crisp. Cool.

Line a serving plate with lettuce leaves. Invert the mold, bowl, or custard cup onto the lettuce-lined plate. Lift and remove mold, bowl, or custard cup. Serve salmon mixture with pita wedges. Makes 8 servings (4 wedges per serving). One serving equals:

   Lean Meat Exchange
▮ **Starch/Bread Exchange**

DILLED GARDEN DIP

Pack vegetables for dipping and this creamy dip in your insulated lunch box for a mid-morning snack.

2   cups low-fat cottage cheese
2   tablespoons tarragon vinegar
1   tablespoon finely chopped green onion
1   tablespoon snipped parsley
1½ teaspoons snipped fresh dill
       or ½ teaspoon dried dillweed
       Dash freshly ground pepper
       Dill sprigs (optional)
4   cups fresh vegetable pieces (broccoli flowerets, carrot sticks, cauliflower flowerets, celery sticks, cherry tomatoes, cucumber slices, green onions, green pepper strips, mushrooms, radishes, *and/or* zucchini slices)

For dip, in a blender container or food processor bowl combine cottage cheese and vinegar. Cover and blend or process till smooth. Transfer cottage cheese mixture to a medium mixing bowl. Stir in green onion, parsley, snipped or dried dill, and pepper. Cover and chill thoroughly.

Transfer dip to a serving bowl. If desired, garnish with fresh dill. Serve with vegetable pieces. Cover and chill any remaining dip up to 1 week. Makes 8 (¼-cup) servings. One serving equals:

■   Lean Meat Exchange
▮   Vegetable Exchange

TOFU-CHEESE CRACKERS

The versatile tofu spread also tastes good stuffed in celery or as a dip for carrot sticks or broccoli flowerets.

4   ounces tofu (bean curd), drained
2   tablespoons grated Parmesan cheese
2   tablespoons finely chopped celery
2   tablespoons finely chopped carrot
1   tablespoon finely chopped green onion
1   tablespoon reduced-calorie mayonnaise
       or salad dressing
¼   teaspoon seasoned salt
       Dash pepper
48 crispy rye crackers

For spread, in a small mixing bowl mash the tofu with a fork. Stir in Parmesan cheese, celery, carrot, green onion, mayonnaise or salad dressing, seasoned salt, and pepper. Cover and chill till serving time. For each serving, top *1 cracker* with *1 teaspoon* of the spread. Cover and chill any remaining spread up to 4 days. Makes 12 servings (4 crackers per serving). One serving equals:

■   Starch/Bread Exchange

PINEAPPLE DIP

2   cups low-fat cottage cheese
1   8-ounce can crushed pineapple (juice pack), drained
¼   cup finely chopped green pepper
       Several dashes bottled hot pepper sauce
2½ cups strawberries, apple slices, pear slices, orange sections, *and/or* banana chunks

Place cottage cheese in a blender container or food processor bowl. Blend or process till smooth. In a mixing bowl mix pureed cottage cheese, pineapple, green pepper, and hot pepper sauce. Cover and chill at least 4 hours. Serve with fresh fruit. Cover and chill any remaining dip up to 3 days. Makes 10 (¼-cup) servings. One serving equals:

■   Meat Exchange
▮   Fruit Exchange

SALSA AND CHIPS

Out of Starch/Bread Exchanges? Serve this tangy dip with celery sticks instead of tortilla wedges.

1 cup seeded, chopped tomatoes (2 small)
2 tablespoons canned diced green chili peppers
1 tablespoon snipped fresh parsley
2 teaspoons red wine vinegar
¼ teaspoon onion powder
⅛ teaspoon salt
⅛ teaspoon garlic powder
2 6-inch flour tortillas

In a blender container or food processor bowl combine tomatoes, chili peppers, parsley, vinegar, onion powder, salt, and garlic powder. Cover and blend or process till nearly smooth. Cover and chill till serving time.

Meanwhile, cut each tortilla into eight wedges. Arrange in a single layer on a baking sheet. Bake in a 350° oven about 15 minutes or till dry and crisp. Cool completely.

Serve toasted tortilla wedges with dip. Cover and chill any remaining dip up to 3 days. Makes 4 (3-tablespoon) servings. One serving equals:

▮ Starch/Bread Exchange
▯ Vegetable Exchange

FAST-FIXIN' SNACK IDEAS

Try these easy-to-fix snacks to keep you on the right track when the hungries attack:

- Use 1 tablespoon peanut butter (1 Lean Meat Exchange and 1 Fat Exchange) to stuff 2 celery stalks (Free Food).
- Sprinkle 3 cups popped (no fat) popcorn (1 Starch/Bread Exchange) with curry powder, oregano, garlic powder, or chili powder (Free Foods) or with 2 tablespoons grated Parmesan cheese (1 Lean Meat Exchange).
- Make an herbed cottage cheese dip by stirring 1 teaspoon dried dillweed, celery seed, or snipped chives (Free Foods) into ¼ cup low-fat cottage cheese (1 Lean Meat Exchange). Serve with 4 crispy rye crackers (1 Bread Exchange).
- Flavor 1 cup carbonated water (Free Food) with lemon juice (Free Food). Or, sip flavored carbonated water. (Check the label to make sure no sugar has been added.)
- Marinate 1 cup sliced cucumber or mushrooms (Free Foods) in 2 tablespoons low-calorie salad dressing (Free Food).
- Wrap lettuce leaves (Free Food) around 1 ounce of mozzarella cheese (1 Lean Meat Exchange and ½ Fat Exchange).
- Combine 1 cup plain nonfat yogurt (1 Milk Exchange) and ½ cup sliced strawberries (½ Fruit Exchange).

CREAMY CHIVE DIP

This cottage cheese dip doubles as a tasty topping for baked potatoes.

1 cup low-fat cottage cheese
2 tablespoons snipped chives
1 teaspoon Worcestershire sauce
⅛ to ¼ teaspoon garlic powder
1½ cups celery sticks, mushrooms, sliced zucchini, *and/or* sliced cucumbers

Place cottage cheese in a blender container or food processor bowl. Cover and blend or process till smooth. Stir in chives, Worcestershire sauce, and garlic powder. Serve as a dip with celery, mushrooms, zucchini, or cucumbers. Cover and chill any remaining dip up to 1 week. Makes 6 (2-tablespoon) servings. One serving equals:

  ■ Lean Meat Exchange

SAVORY POPCORN

Use a hot-air popper (a great investment for a dieter) to pop the corn.

2 teaspoons margarine
3 cups popped popcorn (popped without oil or salt)
¼ teaspoon paprika
⅛ teaspoon garlic salt
⅛ teaspoon ground red pepper

Melt margarine. Drizzle melted margarine over popcorn; toss to coat. Stir together paprika, garlic salt, and ground red pepper. Sprinkle the popcorn with the spice mixture; toss again. Makes 3 (1-cup) servings. One serving equals:

  ■ Bread Exchange
  ▮ Fat Exchange

Nutrition Analysis

	Per Serving									Percent U.S. RDA Per Serving							
	Servings (Per Recipe)	Calories	Protein (g)	Carbohydrate (g)	Total Fat (g)	Saturated Fat (g)	Cholesterol (mg)	Sodium (mg)	Potassium (mg)	Protein	Vitamin A	Vitamin C	Thiamine	Riboflavin	Niacin	Calcium	Iron
Creamy Chive Dip (p. 110)	6	38	5	2	1	0	3	164	90	12	2	5	1	6	2	3	1
Dilled Garden Dip (p. 108)	8	63	9	5	1	1	5	238	206	19	56	35	3	10	3	5	3
Fruit and Yogurt Shake (p. 104)	2	90	4	18	0	0	1	49	377	9	10	13	3	11	3	12	3
Herbed Tomato Juice (p. 105)	6	24	2	5	0	0	0	599	273	4	12	35	3	3	6	2	5
Mexican-Style Hot Chocolate (p. 105)	9	113	8	14	4	2	4	120	413	18	10	2	6	22	1	26	3
Pineapple Dip (p. 108)	10	62	7	7	1	1	4	184	122	14	1	29	3	6	1	4	1
Salmon-Topped Pita Wedges (p. 107)	8	63	6	6	2	0	0	213	113	13	2	1	3	4	9	2	3
Salsa and Chips (p. 109)	4	62	2	12	1	0	0	72	153	4	16	38	3	4	5	3	5
Savory Popcorn (p. 110)	3	24	1	3	1	0	0	58	3	1	3	0	0	0	0	0	1
Tofu-Cheese Crackers (p. 108)	12	106	5	21	1	0	1	294	169	12	7	1	6	4	2	4	7
Veggie Pita Pizzas (p. 107)	4	113	7	15	3	2	8	180	106	15	14	39	8	9	6	13	5

Nutrition and Weight Loss

For a smart weight-reduction diet you must do more than cut out sweets. Sensible diets are 1) varied, 2) balanced, and 3) not too high in calories, fat, cholesterol, and sodium. The diet outlined in this book meets these criteria.

Eat a Varied Diet

No one food group provides all the nutrients you need for good health. That's why the *Eat and Stay Slim* Daily Menu Plans were created. By following the Food Exchanges listed with the Daily Menu Plans, you are assured of a varied and healthy diet.

Eat Nutritionally Balanced Meals

A balanced meal gives you all the nutrients (protein, carbohydrate, fat, vitamins, minerals, water) you need in adequate, but not excessive, amounts. However, the diets of many people, especially women, are often low in two important minerals—calcium and iron. Fiber, although not a nutrient, is typically low in the diets of both men and women.

Calcium. From birth to old age, everyone needs calcium. Even though you stop growing, your bones need calcium to remain healthy. After age 35 or so, bones lose calcium faster than it's replaced. Calcium loss becomes even more critical among women after menopause. With excessive calcium loss, bones become porous and brittle, and are more likely to break, a condition called osteoporosis. Consuming enough calcium throughout adulthood helps protect against osteoporosis.

Foods from the Milk Exchange List, along with cheese from the Meat Exchange List, are the best calcium sources. Each Daily Menu Plan provides the recommended levels of calcium. In addition, a physician may recommend a calcium supplement for postmenopausal women.

Iron. Iron helps carry oxygen in the blood to every body cell, where the oxygen is used to produce energy. If your diet is low in iron, fatigue, weakness, or illness may set in.

For foods high in iron, choose meat and eggs along with poultry and fish from the Meat Exchange List. And eat enriched and whole grains from the Starch/Bread Exchange. Consume fruits and vegetables high in vitamin C, which improves iron absorption.

Even balanced diets may fall short of iron. Because of iron loss during menstruation, many women are at special risk and may benefit from iron supplements. If you feel you are at risk, check with your doctor.

Fiber. Fiber is a carbohydrate that's part of plant foods, but it generally can't be digested. Fiber offers bulk, helping to move waste through the digestive tract. It also helps protect against chronic constipation, intestinal disease, and cancer. Also, some fiber appears to help lower blood cholesterol levels.

High-fiber foods, such as whole grains, dry beans, vegetables, and fruit pulp, have another benefit. They're usually good sources of nutrients, yet relatively low in calories. The amount of fiber in your diet depends on foods you choose from the Starch/Bread, Fruit, and Vegetable Exchange Groups.

Avoid Excess

Many of today's chronic health problems are associated with consuming too many calories and too much fat, cholesterol, and sodium. For good health, practice moderation.

Calories. Carbohydrates and fats provide most of our calories. Protein also contributes calories. In fact, health experts recommend: about 55 percent of total calories from carbohydrates, about 30 percent of total calories from fats, and about 15 percent from protein. Since the Daily Menu Plans were developed using these guidelines, your calories will be healthfully divided among the different sources.

Fat and Cholesterol. Like other nutrients, fat is essential to health. High-fat diets, however, are linked to cardiovascular disease, breast and colon cancers, and obesity. Eating too much saturated fat and cholesterol may help raise blood cholesterol levels. High blood cholesterol can cause arteries to narrow, and eventually can lead to heart attacks. So, nutrition experts make these recommendations for adults: 1) Eat 30 percent or less of total calories as fat, and 2) eat no more than 300 milligrams of cholesterol daily.

The Daily Menu Plans on pages 15–18 limit fat to healthy levels. When possible, choose unsaturated fats rather than saturated fats. Saturated fats come mainly from animal sources of food, hydrogenated fats, and foods made from certain vegetable oils—coconut, palm, and palm kernel oils. Cholesterol is found only in foods of animal origin.

To control saturated fats and cholesterol in your diet, choose lean meats, fish, poultry without skin, and low-fat dairy products. Choose processed foods made with canola, corn, olive, peanut, safflower, and soybean oils. And avoid eating more than the allotted Fat Exchanges. Also, if you need to watch cholesterol, limit high-cholesterol foods, such as shrimp and egg yolks.

Sodium. You need some sodium in your diet to help maintain the balance of fluids that help nutrients pass into your cells and wastes pass out. For adults, consuming 1,100 to 3,300 milligrams of sodium daily is considered adequate. Many Americans consume two to three times that amount.

Consuming too much sodium is a health risk for those with high blood pressure, a condition affecting one in four adults. If you have a family history of high blood pressure, you should consider cutting down on sodium. Start by removing salt from your table and cooking with herbs, rather than salt. Also, limit your consumption of high-sodium processed foods.

The Ups and Downs of Weight Loss

Sometimes dieting doesn't seem fair. Some weeks, even though you've been very careful, you may not lose a pound. Other times, weight may seem to slide off. Why?

While diets can be standardized, people can't be. Losing weight is an individual matter. And many factors affect the speed of reducing.

Many people seem to lose weight more quickly during the first month. That rapid weight loss may, in part, be due to loss of fluids. After a few weeks, body weight often hits a plateau. The body has adapted to receiving fewer calories so pounds come off at a slower rate.

If you're like most people, your weight will fluctuate, up a little today, down a little tomorrow. If you've been carefully following your diet, this weight fluctuation probably reflects changes in your body's balance of fluids. Your body may retain fluids when you eat more salty foods and women retain more fluids at certain times during their menstrual cycles. Every pint of retained fluid weighs about one pound, so retention of fluids can hide the loss of body fat.

In spite of the ups and downs of weight loss, patience and stick-to-itiveness pay off over a period of time. Follow your Daily Menu Plan, and eventually your weight will come down.

Exercise

Exercise is as important to weight control as diet. Pounds pile up from lack of exercise. In fact, studies show that overweight people often eat less than normal-weight people. Exercise makes the difference. Step up your activity and you'll burn more calories.

Weight-bearing exercise, such as brisk walking, jogging, and aerobic dancing, helps build bone strength. Stronger bones reduce the risk of osteoporosis. Doing an aerobic exercise, such as brisk walking, bicycling, swimming, or jogging, at least 20 minutes three times weekly, helps keep the heart muscle strong. And, it also helps lower blood cholesterol levels and relieves stress.

Regular workouts also improve a person's appearance. A flabby body will become firmer and slimmer.

Plan a Smart Exercise Program

Regular exercise is far better than occasional bursts of strenuous activity. A safe, effective exercise session has three phases:

- **Warm up** with five to 10 minutes of stretching or walking. You'll reduce the risk of injury and exercise more efficiently.
- **Work out** intensely for 20 to 30 minutes. Progress slowly so you don't strain yourself. Pace yourself; a good workout shouldn't completely drain you.
- **Cool down,** as you warmed up. If you stop abruptly, you may feel faint or dizzy.

Find the Right Activities

Choose an activity you enjoy so exercise is a pleasant experience and becomes a habit. If you're over 35, check with your doctor before starting an exercise regimen.

Different exercises offer different benefits. You'll benefit most from a variety that builds strength (sit-ups, push-ups), flexibility (stretching, toe touches), and endurance (aerobic dance routines, brisk walking).

The number of calories you burn depends on the type of exercise, the duration, and the intensity of the exercise. Refer to the chart (*below*) to see how exercises differ.

Be active whenever you can. For example, use stairs rather than the elevator or park farther away from your destination and walk.

EXERCISE COMPARISON CHART

Different exercise activities burn different amounts of calories. Use this chart as a guideline in selecting an exercise that you enjoy.

Activity	Calories Burned Per Hour
Lying down, sitting	70 to 100
Office work, domestic chores, driving	120 to 180
Walking, bicycling (moderate speed)	200 to 220
Golf, heavy house-work, bowling, walking (briskly)	250 to 300
Volleyball, skating, jogging, aerobic danc-ing, tennis, swimming	350 to 450
Running, rowing, competitive swimming	600 +

Source: American Medical Association

How to Stay Slim

Congratulations! You've reached your target weight. Now you need to maintain it. Remember: Unwanted pounds can creep up on you. And, they're harder to lose than to gain. The key to weight maintenance is eating the same number of calories your body burns—not more or less.

Stay slim by using the Food Exchange system to guide your eating habits. Besides providing a good weight-loss plan, Food Exchanges offer a reliable, workable approach for weight maintenance. Here's how:

- Determine how many calories you need for weight maintenance. If you're moderately active, figure 15 calories per pound. A 125-pound person needs about 1,875 calories per day to maintain that weight.
- Choose a Daily Menu Plan that is slightly less than or equal to the number of calories you need for maintenance. If your goal is 1,875 calories, follow the 1,800-calorie plan.
- If your calorie goal exceeds the number of calories in the Daily Menu Plan you have selected, add Food Exchanges to the plan to equal your target. For example, if your target is 1,875 calories, add 75 calories in Food Exchanges to the 1,800-calorie plan. The chart (right) lists the calorie values of one exchange in each Exchange Group.
- When you add extra exchanges, choose wholesome foods. For example, one ounce of mozzarella cheese, a Medium-Fat Meat Exchange, added to your sandwich gives you an additional 75 calories. Or, increase your serving size to make up the difference.
- If your calorie goal is much higher—perhaps 2,400 calories (the number of calories to maintain the weight of a 160-pound, moderately active man)—follow the 1,800-calorie plan. Then, add servings from a variety of the Exchange Groups.

MAINTENANCE TIPS

As a quick summary, maintain your new lower weight by following these guidelines.

- Follow the Daily Menu Plan that matches your maintenance needs, perhaps 1,500 or 1,800 calories. Add extra exchanges only if they fit your calorie goal.
- Exercise regularly, at least 20 minutes three times per week.
- Weigh yourself each week. If you've gained a pound or two, cut back on your calorie intake or increase your activity level until you're back at target weight.
- Make your new eating patterns a long-term habit—you'll stay slim for a lifetime.

CALORIE VALUES FOR FOOD EXCHANGE GROUPS

Use this chart to add exchanges to your Daily Menu Plan, if necessary. Add enough exchanges to equal the calories in your daily calorie target.

Exchange	Calories
Starch/Bread	80
Lean Meat	55
Medium-Fat Meat	75
High-Fat Meat	100
Vegetable	25
Fruit	60
Skim Milk	90
Low-Fat Milk	120
Whole Milk	150
Fat	45

Food Exchange Lists

These charts list the foods in each Exchange Group. Each group has a color symbol so you can recognize it easily in the Daily Menu Plans and in the exchanges that follow each recipe. In the lists, tablespoon is abbreviated as "Tbsp." and teaspoon as "tsp."

Lean Meats

Unless otherwise noted, an exchange is 1 ounce of cooked meat trimmed of separable fat. Choose the items on this list often, since most are lower in saturated fat and cholesterol than Medium-Fat or High-Fat Meat Exchanges.

BEEF
round steak	tenderloin
sirloin steak	chipped beef
flank steak	

PORK
fresh ham	Canadian bacon
canned, cured,	tenderloin
or boiled ham	

VEAL
all cuts, except for ground or cubed cutlets

POULTRY (without skin)
chicken	Cornish hen
turkey	

WILD GAME
venison	pheasant, duck,
rabbit	or goose
squirrel	(without skin)

FISH AND SEAFOOD
all fresh or frozen fish
clams, crab, lobster, scallops, shrimp, fresh or canned in water (2 ounces)
oysters, fresh (6 medium)
tuna, canned in water (¼ cup)
herring, uncreamed or smoked
sardines, canned (2 medium)

CHEESE
cottage cheese (¼ cup)
Parmesan cheese (2 Tbsp.)
diet cheeses with less than 55 calories per ounce

OTHER
95% fat-free luncheon meat
egg whites (3)
egg substitutes with less than 55 calories per ¼ cup (¼ cup)

Medium-Fat Meats

Unless otherwise noted, an exchange of the following meats is 1 ounce of cooked meat trimmed of separable fat. Because these items contain more fat than those on the Lean Meat list, one serving counts as 1 Lean Meat Exchange plus ½ Fat Exchange.

BEEF
ground
rib, chuck, or rump roast
cubed, porterhouse, or T-bone steak
meat loaf

PORK
chops	Boston butt
loin roast	cutlets

LAMB
chops	roast
leg	

continued

Medium-Fat Meat List, *continued*

▌VEAL
ground
cubed, unbreaded cutlet

▌POULTRY
chicken (with skin)
domestic goose or duck,
    drained of fat
ground turkey

▌FISH
tuna, canned in oil, drained
    (¼ cup)
salmon, canned
    (¼ cup)

▌CHEESE
ricotta (¼ cup)
mozzarella
other skim or part-skim milk cheeses
diet cheeses with 56–80
    calories per ounce

▌OTHER
86% fat-free luncheon meat
egg (1)
egg substitutes with 56–80
    calories per ¼ cup (¼ cup)
tofu (2½ x 2¾ x 1-inch piece)
liver
heart
kidney
sweetbreads

High-Fat Meats

Unless otherwise noted, an exchange of the following meats is 1 ounce of cooked meat trimmed of separable fat. Because these items contain more fat than those on the Lean Meat or Medium-Fat Meat lists, one serving counts as 1 Lean Meat Exchange plus 1 Fat Exchange.

■ BEEF
prime rib
corned beef
USDA prime cuts

■ PORK
spareribs
ground pork
pork sausage

■ LAMB
ground lamb

■ FISH AND SEAFOOD
any fried product

■ CHEESE
all regular cheeses, such as
    American, Blue, cheddar,
    Monterey Jack, Swiss, etc.

■ OTHER
bologna
salami
pimiento loaf
Polish or Italian
    sausage
knockwurst
bratwurst
turkey or chicken
    frankfurter (1)
peanut butter
    (1 Tbsp.)

This group contains a wide variety of foods, so serving sizes per exchange vary. Most of the items count as 1 Starch/Bread Exchange. But, the items listed under "Starch/Bread Foods Containing Fat" count as 1 Starch/Bread Exchange and 1 Fat Exchange. For unlisted items, ½ cup of cereal, grain, or pasta, or 1 ounce of a bread product is one exchange.

■ CEREALS/GRAINS/PASTA
concentrated bran cereals..... ⅓ cup
flaked bran cereals .... ½ cup
bulgur, cooked .... ½ cup
cooked cereals......................... ½ cup
cornmeal .... 2½ Tbsp.
Grape Nuts cereal .... 3 Tbsp.
grits, cooked............................ ½ cup
other ready-to-eat
    unsweetened cereals .... ¾ cup
pasta, cooked .... ½ cup
puffed cereal .... 1½ cups
rice, white or
    brown, cooked .... ⅓ cup
shredded wheat .... ½ cup
wheat germ............................. 3 Tbsp.

■ DRIED BEANS/PEAS/LENTILS
beans and peas (such as
    kidney, white, split,
    black-eyed), cooked............. ⅓ cup
baked beans .... ¼ cup
lentils, cooked .... ⅓ cup

■ STARCHY VEGETABLES
acorn or butternut
    squash................................... ¾ cup
corn.. ½ cup
corn on the cob 6-inch
lima beans............................... ½ cup
peas.. ½ cup
plantain................................... ½ cup
potato, baked .... 3 ounces
potatoes, mashed.................... ½ cup
sweet potato or yam, plain.... ⅓ cup

■ BREAD
bagel .... ½
bread sticks, crisp,
    4x½-inch 2
croutons, low-fat..................... 1 cup
English muffin .... ½
frankfurter or
    hamburger bun.................. ½
pita, 6-inch diameter.............. ½
dinner roll, small 1
tortilla, 6-inch diameter 1
raisin bread, unfrosted .... 1 slice
rye or pumpernickel
    bread................................... 1 slice
white bread (including
    French and Italian)............ 1 slice
whole wheat bread................ 1 slice

■ CRACKERS/SNACKS
animal crackers...................... 8
graham crackers,
    2½-inch square.................. 3
matzoth .... ¾ ounce
melba toast .... 5 slices
oyster crackers 24
popcorn, popped
    without fat .... 3 cups
pretzels................................... ¾ ounce
crisp rye crackers,
    2x3½ inches........................ 4
saltine crackers 6
whole wheat crackers,
    no fat added .... ¾ ounce

■ ■ STARCH/BREAD FOODS CONTAINING FAT
biscuit, 2½-inch diameter 1
chow mein nooodles............... ½ cup
corn bread, 2-inch cube.......... 2 ounces
French fried potatoes,
    2 to 3½ inches long............ 10
muffin, plain, small 1
pancake, 4-inch diameter 2
rich round crackers............... 6
bread stuffing, prepared........ ¼ cup
taco shell, 6-inch diameter.... 2
waffle, 4½-inch square 1
whole wheat crackers
    containing fat .... 1 ounce

Fruits

For Fruit Exchanges, choose fresh, dried, or unsweetened canned or frozen fruit. For fruits not listed, allow ½ cup fresh fruit or fruit juice or ¼ cup dried fruit for 1 Fruit Exchange.

■ FRESH, FROZEN, CANNED

apple, raw, 2-inch diameter 1
applesauce, unsweetened .... ½ cup
apricots, fresh, medium 4
apricots, canned .... ½ cup
apricot halves, canned 4
banana, 9 inches long .... ½
blackberries, raw .... ¾ cup
blueberries, raw .... ¾ cup
cantaloupe, 5-inch diameter .... ⅓
cantaloupe cubes .... 1 cup
cherries, large, raw 12
cherries, canned .... ½ cup
fruit cocktail, canned .... ½ cup
grapefruit, medium .... ½
grapefruit segments .... ¾ cup
grapes, small 15
honeydew melon, medium .... ⅛
honeydew melon cubes .... 1 cup
kiwi, large 1
mandarin oranges, canned ...... ¾ cup
mango, small .... ½
nectarine, 1½-inch diameter ... 1
orange, 2½-inch diameter 1
papaya, sliced .... 1 cup
peach, 2¾-inch diameter 1
peaches, canned slices .... ½ cup
peaches, canned halves .... 2 halves
pear .... 1 small
pears, canned slices .... ½ cup
pears, canned halves .... 2 halves
persimmon, medium 2
pineapple, fresh .... ¾ cup
pineapple, canned .... ⅓ cup
plum, 2-inch diameter 2
pomegranate .... ½
raspberries, fresh .... 1 cup
strawberries, fresh, whole .... 1¼ cups
tangerine, 2½-inch diameter .. 2
watermelon cubes .... 1¼ cups

■ DRIED FRUIT

apples .... 4 rings
apricots .... 7 halves
dates 2½
figs 1½
prunes 3
raisins .... 2 Tbsp.

■ FRUIT JUICE

apple juice/cider .... ½ cup
cranberry juice cocktail .... ⅓ cup
grapefruit juice .... ½ cup
grape juice .... ⅓ cup
orange juice .... ½ cup
pineapple juice .... ½ cup
prune juice .... ⅓ cup

Vegetables

For Vegetable Exchanges, choose fresh, frozen, or canned vegetables. Unless otherwise noted, the serving size for 1 Vegetable Exchange is ½ cup cooked or canned vegetables or 1 cup raw vegetables.

■ FRESH, FROZEN, CANNED

artichoke (½ medium)
asparagus
beans (green, wax, or Italian)
bean sprouts
beets
broccoli
brussels sprouts
cabbage, cooked
carrots
cauliflower
eggplant
greens (collard, mustard, turnip)
kohlrabi
leeks
mushrooms, cooked
okra
onions
pea pods   *continued*

Vegetable List, *continued*
peppers (green or sweet red)
rutabagas
sauerkraut
spinach, cooked
summer squash (crookneck)
tomato (1 large)
tomato or vegetable juice (½ cup)
turnips
water chestnuts
zucchini, cooked

Milk

The calories and fat in Milk Exchanges vary. The list is divided into three parts—skim and very low-fat milk, low-fat milk, and whole milk. The Daily Menu Plans use skim and very low-fat products. Count a serving of these products as 1 Milk Exchange. If you choose a low-fat milk item, count 1 Milk Exchange and ½ Fat Exchange. Count a serving from the whole milk group as 1 Milk Exchange plus 1 Fat Exchange.

■ SKIM AND VERY LOW-FAT MILK
skim milk .... 1 cup
½ or 1 percent milk .... 1 cup
low-fat buttermilk .... 1 cup
evaporated skim milk .... ½ cup
dry nonfat milk .... ⅓ cup
plain nonfat yogurt .... 8 ounces

■■ LOW-FAT MILK
2 percent milk .... 1 cup
plain low-fat yogurt .... 8 ounces

■■■ WHOLE MILK
whole milk .... 1 cup
evaporated whole milk .... ½ cup
whole plain yogurt .... 8 ounces

Fats

All fats are high in calories, so the serving size per exchange is small. Remember to limit saturated fats.

■ UNSATURATED FATS
avocado .... ⅛ medium
margarine .... 1 tsp.
margarine, diet .... 1 Tbsp.
mayonnaise .... 1 tsp.
reduced-calorie
    mayonnaise .... 1 Tbsp.
almonds, dry-roasted .... 6 whole
cashews, dry-roasted .... 1 Tbsp.
peanuts .... 20 small
pecans .... 2 whole
walnuts .... 2 whole
other nuts .... 1 Tbsp.
seeds, pine nuts,
    sunflower nuts .... 1 Tbsp.
pumpkin seeds .... 2 tsp.
oil (corn, cottonseed,
    safflower, soybean,
    sunflower, olive, peanut).. 1 tsp.
olives .... 10 small
salad dressing,
    mayonnaise-type .... 2 tsp.
salad dressing,
    mayonnaise-type,
    reduced-calorie .... 1 Tbsp.
salad dressing (all
    varieties) .... 1 Tbsp.
salad dressing,
    reduced-calorie .... 2 Tbsp.

■ SATURATED FATS
bacon .... 1 slice
butter .... 1 tsp.
coconut, shredded .... 2 Tbsp.
liquid nondairy creamer ...... 2 Tbsp.
powdered nondairy
    creamer .... 4 tsp.
cream, light .... 2 Tbsp.
dairy sour cream .... 2 Tbsp.
whipping cream .... 1 Tbsp.
cream cheese .... 1 Tbsp.
salt pork .... ¼ ounce

Free

These foods cointain less than 20 calories per serving. You may eat as much as you desire of the items listed without a serving size. However, limit yourself to two or three servings per day of the items listed with a specific serving size.

DRINKS
bouillon or broth without fat
sugar-free carbonated drinks
carbonated water
club soda
cocoa powder, unsweetened (1 Tbsp.)
coffee
drink mixes, sugar-free
tea
tonic water, sugar-free

FRUIT
cranberries (½ cup)
rhubarb (½ cup)

VEGETABLES (raw, 1 cup)
cabbage
celery
Chinese cabbage
cucumber
green onion
hot peppers
mushrooms
radishes
zucchini

SALAD GREENS
endive
escarole
lettuce
romaine
spinach

SWEET SUBSTITUTES
candy, hard, sugar-free
gelatin, sugar-free
gum, sugar-free
jam or jelly, sugar-free (2 tsp.)
pancake syrup, sugar-free (2 Tbsp.)

sugar substitutes (saccharin, aspartame)
whipped topping (2 Tbsp.)

CONDIMENTS
catsup (1 tablespoon)
horseradish
mustard
dill pickles, unsweetened
salad dressing, low-calorie (2 Tbsp.)
taco sauce (1 Tbsp.)
vinegar

OTHER
bottled hot pepper sauce
flavoring extracts (vanilla, almond, peppermint, etc.)
garlic
garlic powder
herbs and spices
lemon
lemon juice
lime
lime juice
nonstick spray coating
onion powder
pimiento
soy sauce
wine, used in cooking (¼ cup)
Worcestershire sauce

The Exchange Lists are the basis of a meal planning system designed by a committee of the American Diabetes Association and The American Dietetic Association. While designed primarily for people with diabetes and others who must follow special diets, the Exchange Lists are based on principles of good nutrition that apply to everyone.

Exchanges for Packaged Foods

Packaged foods are convenient and speedy-to-use for busy dieters. This chart lists Food Exchanges for packaged foods, prepared according to package directions. Serving size is given after each product name.

BIRDS EYE Cheese Sauce Combination Vegetables

Baby Brussels Sprouts with Cheese Sauce (4.5 ounces)........■ starch/bread, ▧ vegetable, ■ fat

Broccoli and Cauliflower with Creamy Italian Cheese Sauce (5 ounces)........ ■ starch/bread, ▧ vegetable, ■ fat

Broccoli with Cheese Sauce (5 ounces)........■ starch/bread, ▧ vegetable, ■ fat

Broccoli with Creamy Italian Cheese Sauce (4.5 ounces)........■ starch/bread, ▧ vegetable, ■ fat

Broccoli, Cauliflower, and Carrots with Cheese Sauce (5 ounces)........■ starch/bread, ▧ vegetable, ■ fat

Cauliflower with Cheese Sauce (5 ounces)........■ starch/bread, ▧ vegetable, ■ fat

Peas and Pearl Onions with Cheese Sauce (5 ounces)........■ starch/bread, ▧ vegetable, ■ fat

BIRDS EYE Combination Vegetables

Broccoli, Carrots, and Pasta Twists (3.3 ounces)........■ starch/bread, ▧ vegetable, ■ fat

Corn, Green Beans, and Pasta Curls (3.3 ounces)........■ starch/bread, ■ fat

Creamed Spinach (3 ounces)........▧ vegetable, ■ fat

French Green Beans with Toasted Almonds (3 ounces)........▧ ▧ vegetable

Green Peas and Pearl Onions (3.3 ounces)........■ starch/bread

Green Peas with Cream Sauce (2.6 ounces)........■ starch/bread, ■ fat

Mixed Vegetables with Onion Sauce (2.6 ounces)........■ starch/bread, ▧ vegetable, ■ fat

Rice and Green Peas with Mushrooms (2.3 ounces)........■ ■ starch/bread

Small Onions with Cream Sauce (3 ounces)........■ starch/bread, ▧ vegetable, ■ fat

BIRDS EYE International Recipes Vegetables With Seasoned Sauces

Bavarian Style Green Beans and Spaetzle (3.3 ounces)........■ starch/bread, ▧ vegetable, ■ fat

Chinese Style (3.3 ounces)........▧ ▧ vegetable, ■ fat

Italian Style (3.3 ounces)........■ starch/bread, ▧ vegetable, ■ fat

Japanese Style (3.3 ounces)........▧ ▧ vegetable, ■ fat

New England Style (3.3 ounces)........■ starch/bread, ▧ vegetable, ■ fat

San Francisco Style (3.3 ounces)........■ starch/bread, ▧ vegetable, ■ fat

BIRDS EYE International Rice Recipes

French Style (3.3 ounces)........■ ■ starch/bread, ■ ■ fat

Italian Style (3.3 ounces)........■ ■ starch/bread, ■ ■ fat

Spanish Style (3.3 ounces)........■ ■ starch/bread, ■ ■ fat

BREYER'S Ice Cream

Any flavor (½ cup)........■ starch/bread, ■ ■ fat

CAMPBELL'S Chunky Soups

Chunky Beef (10¾ ounces)........ lean meat, ■ starch/bread, ■ vegetable, ■ fat

Chunky Chicken Noodle with Mushrooms (10¾ ounces)........ lean meat, ■ starch/bread, ■ vegetable, ■ fat

Chunky Chili Beef (11 ounces)........ lean meat, ■ ■ starch/bread, ■ vegetable, ■ fat

Chunky Clam Chowder (Manhattan) (10¾ ounces)........■ starch/bread, ■ vegetable, ■ fat

Chunky Clam Chowder (New England) (10¾ ounces)........■ starch/bread, ■ vegetable, ■ ■ ■ fat

Chunky Old Fashioned Chicken (10¾ ounces)........ lean meat, ■ starch/bread, ■ vegetable, ■ fat

Chunky Old Fashioned Vegetable Beef (10¾ ounces)........ lean meat, ■ starch/bread, ■ vegetable, ■ fat

Chunky Sirloin Burger (10¾ ounces)........ lean meat, ■ starch/bread, ■ vegetable, ■ ■ fat

Chunky Split Pea and Ham (10¾ ounces)........ lean meat, ■ ■ starch/bread, ■ vegetable, ■ fat

Chunky Vegetable (10¾ ounces)........■ starch/bread, ■ ■ vegetable, ■ fat

CAMPBELL'S Condensed Soups

Bean with Bacon (8 ounces)........ lean meat, ■ starch/bread, ■ vegetable

Beef Noodle (8 ounces)........■ starch/bread

Beefy Mushroom (8 ounces)........■ starch/bread

Cream of Asparagus (8 ounces)........■ starch/bread, ■ fat

Cream of Celery (8 ounces)........■ starch/bread, ■ fat

Cream of Chicken (8 ounces)........■ starch/bread, ■ fat

Cream of Mushroom (8 ounces)........■ starch/bread, ■ fat

Cream of Potato (made with milk) (8 ounces)........■ starch/bread, ■ milk

Cheddar Cheese (8 ounces)........■ starch/bread, ■ fat

Chicken Broth (8 ounces)........■ starch/bread

Chicken Gumbo (8 ounces)........■ starch/bread

Chicken Noodle (8 ounces)........■ starch/bread

Chicken Vegetable (8 ounces)........■ starch/bread

French Onion (8 ounces)........■ starch/bread

Gazpacho (8 ounces)........ ■ starch/bread

Green Pea (8 ounces)........ lean meat, ■ starch/bread, vegetable

Minestrone (8 ounces)........ ■ starch/bread

Nacho Cheese (made with water) (8 ounces)........ starch/bread, ■ fat

Split Pea with Ham and Bacon (8 ounces)........ lean meat, ■ starch/bread, vegetable

Tomato (8 ounces)........ ■ starch/bread

Tomato (made with whole milk) (10¾ ounces)........ ■ starch/bread, milk

Vegetable Beef (10¾ ounces)........ ■ starch/bread

DINTY MOORE Products

Beef Stew........ lean meat, ■ starch/bread, ■ fat

Vegetable Stew........ ■ starch/bread, vegetable, ■ fat

Noodles and Chicken........ lean meat, ■ starch/bread, ■ ■ fat

D-ZERTA Pudding

Reduced-Calorie Pudding (prepared with skim milk)
Butterscotch, Chocolate, Vanilla (½ cup)........ ■ starch/bread, milk

FRANCO AMERICAN Products

Au Jus Gravy (2 ounces)........ free

Beef Gravy (2 ounces)........ ■ fat

Chicken Gravy (2 ounces)........ ■ fat

GREEN GIANT Vegetables

Broccoli, Cauliflower, Carrots in Butter Sauce (½ cup)........ vegetable

Broccoli Spears in Butter Sauce (½ cup)........ vegetable, ■ fat

Brussels Sprouts in Butter Sauce (½ cup)........ ■ vegetable

Corn in Butter Sauce (½ cup)........ ■ starch/bread, ■ fat

Cut Green Beans in Butter Sauce (½ cup)........ vegetable

Cut Leaf Spinach in Butter Sauce (½ cup)........ ■ vegetable, ■ fat

Rice and Broccoli in Flavored Cheese Sauce (½ cup)........ ■ starch/bread, vegetable, ■ fat

Rice Pilaf (½ cup)........ ■ ■ starch/bread, ■ fat

Sweet Peas in Butter Sauce (½ cup)........ ■ starch/bread, ■ fat

Three Bean Salad (½ cup)........ ■ starch/bread

HÄAGEN DAZS Ice Cream Desserts

Ice Cream—chocolate or vanilla (½ cup)........ ■ starch/bread, milk, ■ ■ ■ fat

Ice Cream Bar—chocolate or vanilla with dark chocolate coating (1 each)........
■ ■ starch/bread, ■ ■ ■ ■ fat

JELL-O Pudding

Sugar-free *instant* pudding (all flavors) prepared with skim or 2% milk (½ cup)........
■ starch/bread, milk

Sugar-free *regular* pudding (all flavors) prepared with skim or 2% milk (½ cup)........
■ starch/bread, milk

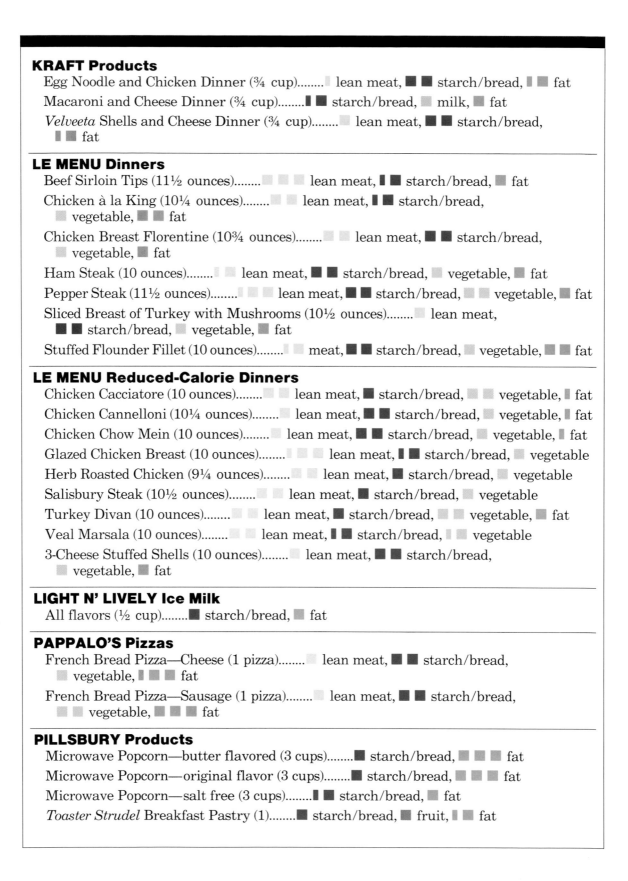

KRAFT Products

Egg Noodle and Chicken Dinner (¾ cup)........ lean meat, starch/bread, fat

Macaroni and Cheese Dinner (¾ cup)........ starch/bread, milk, fat

Velveeta Shells and Cheese Dinner (¾ cup)........ lean meat, starch/bread, fat

LE MENU Dinners

Beef Sirloin Tips (11½ ounces)........ lean meat, starch/bread, fat

Chicken à la King (10¼ ounces)........ lean meat, starch/bread, vegetable, fat

Chicken Breast Florentine (10¾ ounces)........ lean meat, starch/bread, vegetable, fat

Ham Steak (10 ounces)........ lean meat, starch/bread, vegetable, fat

Pepper Steak (11½ ounces)........ lean meat, starch/bread, vegetable, fat

Sliced Breast of Turkey with Mushrooms (10½ ounces)........ lean meat, starch/bread, vegetable, fat

Stuffed Flounder Fillet (10 ounces)........ meat, starch/bread, vegetable, fat

LE MENU Reduced-Calorie Dinners

Chicken Cacciatore (10 ounces)........ lean meat, starch/bread, vegetable, fat

Chicken Cannelloni (10¼ ounces)........ lean meat, starch/bread, vegetable, fat

Chicken Chow Mein (10 ounces)........ lean meat, starch/bread, vegetable, fat

Glazed Chicken Breast (10 ounces)........ lean meat, starch/bread, vegetable

Herb Roasted Chicken (9¼ ounces)........ lean meat, starch/bread, vegetable

Salisbury Steak (10½ ounces)........ lean meat, starch/bread, vegetable

Turkey Divan (10 ounces)........ lean meat, starch/bread, vegetable, fat

Veal Marsala (10 ounces)........ lean meat, starch/bread, vegetable

3-Cheese Stuffed Shells (10 ounces)........ lean meat, starch/bread, vegetable, fat

LIGHT N' LIVELY Ice Milk

All flavors (½ cup)........ starch/bread, fat

PAPPALO'S Pizzas

French Bread Pizza—Cheese (1 pizza)........ lean meat, starch/bread, vegetable, fat

French Bread Pizza—Sausage (1 pizza)........ lean meat, starch/bread, vegetable, fat

PILLSBURY Products

Microwave Popcorn—butter flavored (3 cups)........ starch/bread, fat

Microwave Popcorn—original flavor (3 cups)........ starch/bread, fat

Microwave Popcorn—salt free (3 cups)........ starch/bread, fat

Toaster Strudel Breakfast Pastry (1)........ starch/bread, fruit, fat

POST Cereals

Bran Flakes (1 ounce)........■ starch/bread

Corn Flakes (1 ounce)........▌■ starch/bread

Fortified Oat Flakes (1 ounce)........▌■ starch/bread

Fruit & Fibre (1 ounce—all varieties)........■ starch/bread

Granola (1 ounce)........■ starch/bread, ■ fat

Grape-Nuts (1 ounce)........▌■ starch/bread

Grape-Nuts Flakes (1 ounce)........▌■ starch/bread

Raisin Bran (1 ounce)........▌ starch/bread, ▌ fruit

PREGO Spaghetti Sauce

Extra Chunky Sauce with mushroom, green pepper, tomato and/or onion (4 ounces)........
▌ starch/bread, ■ vegetable, ■ fat

Spaghetti Sauce (4 ounces)........■ starch/bread, ■ vegetable, ■ fat

Spaghetti Sauce, Marinara Style (4 ounces)........▌ starch/bread, ■ vegetable, ■ fat

STOUFFER'S RIGHT COURSE Entrées

Beef Dijon with Pasta and Vegetables (9½ ounces)........■ lean meat, ■ ■ starch/bread,
■ vegetable

Beef Ragout with Rice Pilaf (10 ounces)........■ lean meat, ■ ■ starch/bread,
■ vegetable, ▌ fat

Chicken Italiano with Fettucini and Vegetables (9⅝ ounces)........■ lean meat,
▌■ starch/bread, ■ vegetable, ▌ milk, ▌ fat

Chicken Tenderloins in Barbeque Sauce with Rice Pilaf (8¾ ounces)........■ lean meat,
■ ■ starch/bread, ▌ fat

Chicken Tenderloins in Peanut Sauce with Linguini and Vegetables (9¼ ounces)........
■ ■ ■ lean meat, ▌■ starch/bread, ■ vegetable, ▌ fat

Fiesta Beef with Corn Pasta (8⅞ ounces)........■ lean meat, ■ ■ starch/bread,
■ vegetable

Homestyle Pot Roast (9¼ ounces)........■ lean meat, ■ starch/bread, ■ vegetable, ▌ fat

Sesame Chicken (10 ounces)........■ lean meat, ■ ■ starch/bread, ■ vegetable, ▌ fat

Shrimp Primavera (9⅝ ounces)........■ lean meat, ■ ■ starch/bread, ■ vegetable, ▌ fat

Sliced Turkey in Mild Curry Sauce with Rice Pilaf (8¾ ounces)........■ lean meat,
▌■ starch/bread, ▌ fruit, ■ milk

Vegetarian Chili (9¾ ounces)........▌■ ■ starch/bread, ■ ■ vegetable, ■ fat

TOP SHELF Products

Chili Con Carne Supreme (10.3 ounces)........■ ■ lean meat, ■ ■ starch/bread, ■ fat

Glazed Breast of Chicken (10 ounces)........■ ■ ■ lean meat, ■ ■ ■ ■ vegetable

Italian Style Lasagna (10 ounces)........■ ■ ■ lean meat, ■ starch/bread, ■ ■ vegetable,
▌■ fat

TOP SHELF Products *(continued)*

Lemon Fillet of Cod (10 ounces)........ ■ ■ ■ lean meat, ■ ■ starch/bread, ■ vegetable, ■ ■ fat

Linguini in White Clam Sauce (10 ounces)........■ starch/bread, ■ vegetable, ■ milk, ■ ■ ■ fat

Spaghettini in Meat Sauce (10 ounces)........ ■ lean meat, ■ ■ starch/bread, ■ ■ vegetable, ■ fat

Tender Beef Roast (10 ounces)........ ■ ■ ■ lean meat, ■ starch/bread, ■ ■ ■ vegetable

TOTINO'S Pizzas

Cheese Pizza (one-sixth pizza)........ ■ lean meat, ■ ■ starch/bread, ■ ■ fat

Combination Pizza (one-sixth pizza)........ ■ lean meat, ■ ■ starch/bread, ■ ■ fat

Pepperoni Pizza (one-sixth pizza)........ ■ lean meat, ■ ■ starch/bread, ■ ■ fat

Microwave Pizza—Cheese (4.2 ounces)........ ■ lean meat, ■ ■ starch/bread, ■ ■ fat

Microwave Pizza—Sausage and Pepperoni Combination (4.2 ounces)........ ■ lean meat, ■ ■ starch/bread, ■ ■ ■ fat

VAN DE KAMP'S Frozen Fish

Battered Fish Fillet (1)........ ■ lean meat, ■ starch/bread, ■ ■ fat

Battered Fish Sticks (4)........ ■ lean meat, ■ starch/bread, ■ fat

WEIGHT WATCHER'S Entrées

Beef Salisbury Steak Romana with Rotini Noodles........ ■ lean meat, ■ ■ starch/bread, ■ ■ vegetable, ■ fat

Beef Stroganoff with Parsley Noodles........ ■ ■ lean meat, ■ ■ starch/bread, ■ vegetable, ■ fat

Beefsteak Burritos........ ■ lean meat, ■ ■ starch/bread, ■ vegetable, ■ ■ fat

Breaded Chicken Patty Parmigiana with Vegetable Medley........ ■ ■ lean meat, ■ starch/bread, ■ ■ vegetable, ■ ■ fat

Chicken à la King........ ■ ■ lean meat, ■ starch/bread, ■ vegetable, ■ milk

Chicken Cacciatore with Spaghetti........ ■ ■ lean meat, ■ ■ starch/bread, ■ ■ vegetable

Chicken Nuggets........ ■ lean meat, ■ starch/bread, ■ fat

Fillet of Fish au gratin with Broccoli........ ■ lean meat, ■ starch/bread, ■ vegetable, ■ milk

French Bread Pizza—Cheese .... ■ lean meat, ■ ■ starch/bread, ■ vegetable, ■ ■ fat

Italian Cheese Lasagna with Ricotta, Mozzarella, and Romano Cheeses........ ■ lean meat, ■ ■ starch/bread, ■ vegetable, ■ ■ fat

Pepperoni *or* Sausage Pizza........ ■ lean meat, ■ ■ starch/bread, ■ ■ vegetable, ■ fat

Stuffed Sole with Newburg Sauce........ ■ lean meat, ■ ■ starch/bread, ■ vegetable, ■ skim milk, ■ fat

Veal Patty Parmigiana with Vegetable Medley........ ■ ■ lean meat, ■ starch/bread, ■ vegetable, ■ fat

INDEX

A-B

Apple Rice Pudding, 99
Apricot and Banana Sherbet, 100
Asparagus with Dijon Sauce, 72
Athenian Lamb Kabobs, 65
Baked Cajun Chicken, 20
Barbecued Ham Slice, 59
Beef
   Beef Burgundy, 52
   Beef Slaw-Wiches, 56
   Lime Beef-and-Chicken
    Kabobs, 50
   Mustard-Marinated Steak, 49
   Old-Fashioned Beef Stew, 48
   One-Pot Spaghetti, 56
   Roast Beef with Mushroom
    Sauce, 48
   Round Steak Stroganoff, 53
   Savory Steak and Gravy, 52
   Spaghetti Squash with Tomato
    Sauce, 54
   Steak with Marsala Sauce, 50
   Stir-Fried Beef and Spinach, 54
   Taco Compuesto, 53
   Tijuana Taco Salad, 49
Berry-Sauced Poached Pears, 98
Beverages
   Fruit and Yogurt Shake, 104
   Herbed Tomato Juice, 105
   Mexican-Style Hot
    Chocolate, 105
Blue Cheese Dressing, 77
Bread Pudding, 99
Bulgur and Vegetables, 88
Butternut Squash and Apples, 86

C

Cajun Corn and Okra, 88
Cajun Pork Pinwheels, 61
Calorie-Counter's Coleslaw, 76
Carrots and Pea Pods in Orange
  Sauce, 84

*We analyzed the nutritional
content of each recipe using
the first choice if ingredient
substitutions are given, and
using the first serving size if a
serving range is given. We
omitted optional ingredients
from the analysis.*

Cauliflower-Asparagus
  Stir-Fry, 73
Cheese-Stuffed Chicken
  Breasts, 25
Chef's Salad Bowl, 63
Cherry-Berry Compote, 94
Chicken
   Baked Cajun Chicken, 20
   Cheese-Stuffed Chicken
    Breasts, 25
   Chicken and Broccoli
    Skillet, 23
   Chicken Kabobs with Peanut
    Sauce, 28
   Chinese-Style Chicken, 21
   Country French Chicken, 20
   Fruited Chicken Salad, 35
   Garlic Chicken with Pasta, 31
   Hot Chicken Salad, 23
   Lemon Chicken with Curried
    Rice, 26
   Lime Beef-and-Chicken
    Kabobs, 50
   Mandarin Chicken Dinner, 34
   Orange-Sauced Chicken
    Stir-Fry, 24
   Oriental Chicken Stir-Fry, 28
   Plum-Chicken Stir-Fry, 29
   Quick Chicken Cacciatore, 24
   Spicy Baked Chicken, 21
   Taco Chicken Stew, 34
   Teriyaki Chicken Kabobs, 31
   Turkey Potpie, 33
   Wine-Marinated Chicken, 29
Chilled Poached Fish, 40
Chinese-Style Chicken, 21
Chocolate Cheesecake Bars, 95
Corn-Clam Chowder, 78
Country French Chicken, 20
Creamy Asparagus Soup, 80
Creamy Carrot-Potato Boats, 81
Creamy Chive Dip, 110
Creamy Vegetable Toss, 74
Cucumber-Buttermilk Soup, 79
Curried Orange Rice, 90

D-F

Dilled Garden Dip, 108
Easy Baked Fish, 40
Eggs
   Eggs Florentine, 66
   Salsa-Topped Frittata, 66

Fish
   Chilled Poached Fish, 40
   Easy Baked Fish, 40
   Flounder Dijon, 36
   Garlic-Marinated Swordfish
    Steaks, 36
   Hearty Salmon Pie, 45
   Lemon-Poached Halibut, 39
   Mexican-Style Fish Fillets, 38
   Oriental Fish with Pasta, 39
   Oven-Fried Fish, 38
   Poached Fish with Lime
    Sauce, 41
   Salmon-Topped Pita
    Wedges, 107
   Spinach-Topped Halibut, 41
   Tangy Salmon Salad, 45
   Tuna Bulgur Salad, 46
   Tuna Pockets, 46
   Tuna Toss, 45
Flounder Dijon, 36
Fresh Fruit Medley, 102
Fresh Fruit Plate, 100
Fruit and Yogurt Shake, 104
Fruited Chicken Salad, 35
Fruited Coffee Cake, 94
Fruited Crab Salad, 43
Fruited Ham Toss, 64

G-L

Garlic Chicken with Pasta, 31
Garlic-Marinated Swordfish
  Steaks, 36
Green Beans and Water
  Chestnuts, 73
Ham
   Barbecued Ham Slice, 59
   Chef's Salad Bowl, 63
   Fruited Ham Toss, 64
   Ham Burritos, 64
   Pasta Ham Salad, 61
   Skillet Potato Dinner, 60
   Turkey Ham Pilaf, 33
Hearty Salmon Pie, 45
Herbed Mushrooms, 84
Herbed Rice, 91
Herbed Tomato Juice, 105
Herbed Tomato Soup, 80
Herbed Zucchini, 84
Hot Chicken Salad, 23
Lamb
   Athenian Lamb Kabobs, 65
   Lamb Chops with Peaches, 64
Lean Veal Parmesan, 58

Lemon Chicken with Curried
Rice, 26
Lemon-Poached Halibut, 39
Lime Beef-and-Chicken
Kabobs, 50

M-O

Mandarin Chicken Dinner, 34
Marinated Tomatoes and
Cucumbers, 82
Melon Mousse, 97
Mexican-Style Fish Fillets, 38
Mexican-Style Hot Chocolate, 105
Mint-Chocolate Cream Puffs, 97
Mustard-Marinated Steak, 49
Old-Fashioned Beef Stew, 48
One-Pot Spaghetti, 56
Onion Soup Parmesan, 79
Orange and Berry Parfaits, 95
Orange-Applesauce Muffins, 87
Orange-Sauced Chicken
Stir-Fry, 24
Oriental Chicken Stir-Fry, 28
Oriental Fish with Pasta, 39
Oven-Fried Fish, 38

P-R

Pasta Ham Salad, 61
Pear and Date Crisp, 100
Pepper and Rice Timbales, 91
Pineapple and Pork Stir-Fry, 59
Pineapple Dip, 108
Plum-Chicken Stir-Fry, 29
Poached Fish with Lime
Sauce, 41
Polynesian Shrimp, 44
Pork
Cajun Pork Pinwheels, 61
Pineapple and Pork
Stir-Fry, 59
Pork Medaillons with Apple-
Yogurt Sauce, 63
Spicy Marinated Pork
Chops, 60
Potluck Potato Salad, 76
Pumpkin Chiffon Pudding, 102
Quick Chicken Cacciatore, 24
Roast Beef with Mushroom
Sauce, 48
Round Steak Stroganoff, 53

S

Salmon-Topped Pita Wedges, 107
Salsa and Chips, 109
Salsa-Topped Frittata, 66
Saucy Shrimp with Artichoke
Hearts, 44
Sautéed Peppers and
Tomatoes, 72
Savory Bran Muffins, 87
Savory Popcorn, 110
Savory Steak and Gravy, 52
Seafood
Fruited Crab Salad, 43
Polynesian Shrimp, 44
Saucy Shrimp with Artichoke
Hearts, 44
Stir-Fried Scallops with
Pasta, 43
Skillet Potato Dinner, 60
Slender French Fries, 82
Smoked Turkey Salad, 34
Spaghetti Squash with Tomato
Sauce, 54
Spicy Baked Chicken, 21
Spicy Marinated Pork Chops, 60
Spinach Salad, 77
Spinach-Topped Halibut, 41
Steak with Marsala Sauce, 50
Stir-Fried Beef and Spinach, 54
Stir-Fried Scallops with Pasta, 43
Sweet-and-Sour Sesame
Dressing, 77
Sweet Pepper and Turkey
Rolls, 30
Sweet Potatoes and Pineapple, 86

T-Z

Taco Chicken Stew, 34
Taco Compuesto, 53
Tangy Salmon Salad, 45
Tangy Vegetable Salad, 83
Teriyaki Chicken Kabobs, 31
Tex-Mex Turkey Tenderloins, 26
Tijuana Taco Salad, 49
Tofu and Broccoli Stir-Fry, 65
Tofu-Cheese Crackers, 108
Tropical Fruit Cup, 94
Tuna Bulgur Salad, 46
Tuna Pockets, 46
Tuna Toss, 45
Turkey
Hot Chicken Salad, 23
Lean Veal Parmesan, 58
Oriental Chicken Stir-Fry, 28
Smoked Turkey Salad, 34

Turkey (continued)
Spaghetti Squash with Tomato
Sauce, 54
Sweet Pepper and Turkey
Rolls, 30
Tex-Mex Turkey
Tenderloins, 26
Turkey Ham Pilaf, 33
Turkey Loaf, 30
Turkey Potpie, 33
Turkey Waldorf Salad, 35
Veal
Lean Veal Parmesan, 58
Veal and Peppers Italiano, 58
Veal Chops with Vegetables, 57
Veal Scallopini, 57
Vegetable-Pasta Salad, 74
Vegetable Skillet, 83
Veggie Pita Pizzas, 107
Waldorf Salad, 83
Wild Rice and Mushrooms, 90
Wine-Marinated Chicken, 29
Zesty Tomato Dressing, 77

Tips

Calorie Values for Food Exchange
Groups, 114
Choosing a Salad Dressing, 46
Eating Away From Home, 68
Exercise Comparison Chart, 113
Fast Fixin' Snack Ideas, 109
Five-Spice Powder, 54
Ideal Height and Weight Chart, 7
Low-Calorie Thirst
Quencher, 105
Menu Planning Step-by-Step, 12
Micro-Cooking Poultry, 35
Sugar Substitutes, 98
Sugar Substitutes and Our
Recipes, 99
You Can Fit Snacks into Your
Diet, 104

Have BETTER HOMES AND
GARDENS® magazine delivered to
your door. For information,
write to:
MR. ROBERT AUSTIN
P.O. BOX 4536
DES MOINES, IA 50336